D0611160

juice
liz earle

photography by
georgia glynn-smith

Liz Earle is a leading British beauty and health writer and broadcaster. The bestselling author of more than 30 books focusing on beauty, health, food and wellbeing, Liz has also presented several British lifestyle TV programmes. Known for her natural approach to beauty and wellbeing, she is a founder of the botanical Liz Earle Beauty Co. where she created many of the award-winning skincare products that have become iconic global classics. Liz is also the founder of Liz Earle Wellbeing, the healthy lifestyle website that hosts much of her food and farming writing as well as her campaigns on ethical and sustainability issues. In 2010, Liz founded the charity LiveTwice to offer opportunity and help for the disadvantaged, working in both the UK and in developing countries. She was awarded the MBE for services to the beauty industry by Her Majesty The Queen in 2007 and received an honorary doctorate from Portsmouth University in 2010.

www.lizearlewellbeing.com
The home of Liz Earle Wellbeing

www.lizearle.com
The home of Liz Earle Beauty Co.

First published in Great Britain in 2015 by
Kyle Books, an imprint of Kyle Cathie Ltd
192–198 Vauxhall Bridge Road
London SW1V 1DX
general.enquiries@kylebooks.com
www.kylebooks.com

10 9 8 7 6 5 4 3 2 1

ISBN 978 0 85783 273 3

Text © 2015 Liz Earle
Design © 2015 Kyle Books
Photography © 2015 Georgia Glynn Smith*
Illustrations © 2015 Christopher Noulton
* except pages 31, 38, 85, 88, 93, 95, 109, 150,
168, 192 by Patrick Drummond

Liz Earle is hereby identified as the author of
this work in accordance with Section 77 of the
Copyright, Designs and Patents Act 1988.

All rights reserved. No reproduction, copy or
transmission of this publication may be made
without written permission. No paragraph of
this publication may be reproduced, copied
or transmitted save with written permission
or in accordance with the provisions of the
Copyright Act 1956 (as amended). Any person
who does any unauthorised act in relation
to this publication may be liable to criminal
prosecution and civil claims for damages.

Art Director & Designer: Sinem Erkas
Illustrator: Christopher Noulton
Photographers: Georgia Glynn Smith
& Patrick Drummond
Food Stylist: Emily Jonzen
Prop Stylist: Tamzin Ferdinando
Hair & Make-up: Kerry September
Project Editor: Sophie Allen
Copy Editor: Stephanie Evans
Editorial Assistant: Claire Rogers
Production: Nic Jones, Gemma John
and Lisa Pinnell

A Cataloguing in Publication record for this
title is available from the British Library.

Colour reproduction by ALTA London
Printed and bound in China by C&C Offset
Printing Co., Ltd.

All recipes serve one
and are made with
organic produce

Introduction
p.6

– 1 –
Why juice?
p.8

– 2 –
Getting started
p.34

– 3 –
Juice therapy &
& juice cures
p.82

– 4 –
Juicing for
weight loss
p.96

– 5 –
Juicing for
better skin
p.112

– 6 –
Juicing
for energy
p.132

– 7 –
Juicing
for life
p.148

– 8 –
Juicy foods
p.166

Useful addresses
p.188

Index
p.190

Acknowledgements
p.192

Introduction

Juicing has never been more fashionable, with almost every Hollywood superstar and natural health guru pouring praise on the potency of freshly pressed plant juices. My first book on the subject, *Liz Earle's Quick Guide to Juicing* (on which this book is based), published back in 1995, helped pioneer the subject and – far from being dismissed as yet another food fad – the popularity of juicing has soared, along with the raft of evidence to support its many health benefits. Every celebrity interview we read seems to include a new juicing regime; a host of companies now deliver fresh juice diets direct to our doors and even the local sandwich shop is likely to offer an array of fresh juices instead of the long-life, devitalised juice cartons that were on sale just a few years ago.

I've been singing the praises of juicing for over 30 years and am excited to share with you here in this beautifully photographed book their many varied health, beauty and wellbeing benefits. Juicing is both quick and easy – it's just about the fastest, cheapest and most effective health habit I know. In the next few chapters you'll discover that almost every fruit and vegetable can be used for juicing – and once you start to see (and feel) the benefits, including renewed energy, weight loss, clearer skin and increased vitality, you'll never look back! Juicing is one of the few modern health and beauty techniques that really has stood the test of time.

In *Juice*, you'll find all you need for the most novice beginner to get started as well as more advanced nutritional knowledge and new super-food recipes for the seasoned juicing fan. I'm sharing my favourite, most delicious, tried-and-trusted juicing recipes, split into sections so you can easily find them according to your need.

For the beginner, we'll start with the how-to's and why's of basic juicing techniques, including how to choose your juicer and some comprehensive advice on which fruits and veggies are best for first-time juicing. I've added a complete listing of all the produce you're most likely to want to juice, together with their juice rating, as well as information on many of the newer and more unusual juicing ingredients, from acai seeds to wheat grass.

For the experienced devotee, you'll also find my all-time, best-ever, inner-cleansing juice diets, including one-day and three-day fasting and detoxing programmes. These are some of the most powerful 'juice cures' and you'll find these together with recommended juice recipes for everyday ailments. There's a specific section on juicing for weight loss, with recommended recipes and a suggested healthy eating plan.

Natural fresh juices are also the perfect internal tonic for smoother, clearer skin and I've included special youthful-skin recipes as well as skin cleansing combinations for the most radiant-looking skin.

Juicing is just brilliant for boosting vitality and is an excellent way to increase natural energy levels, especially useful for those of us with hectic, over-stressed lifestyles.

Juicing is something that works for all ages and stages of life, from the first few sips of a baby's juice to nutritious, easy to digest formulas for the elderly or those convalescing after illness. There's no surer way to get back on your feet or to absorb vitality-boosting nutrients in such an easily assimilated form – from the very young to the very old.

Last, but not least, juices are incredibly versatile and useful for any cook, so I've included a selection of my favourite recipes for 'juicy foods', from soups to sauces, muffins and more.

Welcome to the wonderful world of juicing – enjoy the sheer fun and great taste of fresh vitality on its way to you.
Sip Sip Hooray!

Liz Earle, MBE, LL.D

— 1 —

Why
juice?

Fresh juices have the power to nourish, cleanse, protect, soothe and heal. Unprocessed and often unpeeled, you get all the nutritional benefit of fruit and veg in one delicious glass. Once you start to include juices in your daily diet I defy you not to develop a healthy addiction to drinking some form of fresh juice every day.

There has always been much debate about the relationship between healthy eating and freedom from disease. While some people think there is little or no relationship between the two, various naturopaths and dietary experts believe our entire nutritional wellbeing is the pivot on which health and disease balance. We know that many of the chronic, and increasingly prevalent, diseases commonly associated with the typical 'Western' diet, such as colon cancer, high blood pressure and diabetes, are almost unheard of among other cultures with different eating habits. More recently, a diet high in refined sugars and starches (carbohydrates) has been specifically identified as the likely cause of these diseases.

Modern food is becoming less and less healthy as we demand greater economic returns from crops and more refined and processed 'convenience foods'. We're losing sight of the natural product itself. Commercial farming is intensive, competitive and relies on chemical fertilisers and pesticides to sustain high yields. This drive for quantity over quality not only robs the soil of nutrients but also leaves harmful chemical residues in the growing plants. Food processing further depletes and destroys vital nutrients, so

by the time food gets to our table there is far less of the original goodness left. Juicing fresh ingredients can return us to a more natural diet – making the critical difference between being poorly nourished or well-nourished.

While research is continually ongoing in the fields of nutrition and health, many health experts and practitioners believe that nutritional deficiencies are one of the most common contributors to disease and yet they are one of the most easily preventable factors in the modern age. So few of us in the so-called 'developed world' follow a healthy life plan of wholesome, balanced eating and regular exercise that it is scarcely surprising that we suffer from a long list of chronic complaints, ranging from arthritis and diabetes to coronary heart disease and cancer, which affects the quality of our lives and, ultimately, can result in early death.

Health isn't something that can be turned on or off overnight. It is not what we eat or drink occasionally that determines our wellbeing, but what we consume out of habit, every day. That's why it is so important to eat natural, well-balanced foods, directly from nature's garden, not via a processing plant. Drinking fresh fruit and vegetable juices forms a valuable part of the dietary journey back to health and happiness and their greatest benefit is derived when they are combined with a healthy diet, positive thinking, correct breathing and regular exercise.

The fact that juices are so easily digested and assimilated helps to explain why they have such a health-building impact on the body. We can make maximum use of the nutrients, essential vitamins, minerals, amino acids, enzymes and antioxidants they contain at minimum cost to the digestive system. Juices have the power to help protect us from illness by providing high levels of easily absorbed nutrients that are specifically needed to strengthen the immune system. They are a quick and easy way to maximise our nutritional intake to benefit every cell in the body, stimulating our metabolism, while the non-soluble fibre content ensures our gut functions optimally. All these things help to maintain a healthy, vibrant body. So drinking fresh juices is a wonderfully healthy habit to acquire – and it's very simple.

Why not buy fresh juices?

The straight answer is that many so-called 'pure juices' are not what they appear to be! For example, back in 1987 an American juice company pleaded guilty to selling millions of bottles of artificially flavoured water labelled as 100 per cent pure apple juice. While that might seem like an isolated case, juice manufacturers may import cheaper fruit and vegetable produce from countries that are less regulated in their use of fertilisers and pesticides. Minute traces of these chemicals penetrate the growing crop and eventually end up in our bodies. When we buy fruit we can scrub or peel it; or we can buy organic or grow our own. When we buy a ready-prepared juice we are relying on the integrity of the processor.

A second reason not to buy ready-prepared juice is that fresh juices need to be consumed within a couple of hours, otherwise they may lose much of their vitality and nutrients. If a juice is left to stand, enzyme activity is reduced. Enzymes are those substances that help chemical reactions take place in the body, making them vital to proper digestion. How many shop-bought juices are less than a few hours old? In order to give them a longer shelf-life most are pasteurised or sterilised – processes that involve high temperatures, which not only destroy the active enzymes but also some of the nutrients as well, such as vitamin C, effectively rendering them 'dead food'. They may taste pleasant but they aren't doing your body much good.

Third, some ready-made juices contain a host of additives ranging from colourings and flavourings to GM-corn syrup, salt and synthetic preservatives. One of my many personal bugbears are the bottles and cartons of 'juice' that, on closer inspection, are actually a 'juice drink' so always check the label for these weasel-words. Juice drinks are mostly water with added sugar, synthetic flavours and preservatives – and a small amount of actual juice – so be aware! Whilst it is true that some ready-made juices are well-made products, as always, it is a case of being discerning and scrutinising the labels, armed with the knowledge that 'fresh is best'.

The beauty benefits

Beauty, like health, comes from within, so what we eat plays a vital role here. Good skincare can help us look good on the outside, but nothing will last if it doesn't also come from within. Sparkling eyes, clear glowing skin, vim and vigour are all signs of a healthy working system. Raw fruit and vegetable juices aid the body's natural functions of cleansing and repair to keep us looking young and feeling great. They are also bursting with vitamins, minerals and other very valuable micro-nutrients that help build stronger, clearer and more youthful-looking skin. Fruit and vegetables – especially the most colourful kind – are key here. The pigments in fresh produce correlate to the nutritional compounds contained within, for example the orange colour of carrots, apricots and mangoes means a rich source of carotene, whilst the red, purply blue tones of cherries, blueberries and red cabbage come from antioxidant-rich anthocyanins. These nutrients are particularly useful when it comes to preserving our collagen and elastin fibres, the springy network of elastic tissues that gives skin its youthful plumped-up glow.

It's really not surprising that juices have become so popular when we consider how well they can help us to achieve optimum health and vitality, while also keeping us looking more youthful – and radiant.

Juices vs. smoothies

Juicing is a fantastic way to extract nutrients from fresh fruits and vegetables, along with the water content, to produce a nutritionally rich and concentrated drink. Because the fibre is removed during the juicing process, our digestive system does not have to work as hard to break down the food to release available nutrients. By contrast, smoothies and other 'mashed' fruit and vegetable makers include the fibre content, which slows down the release of nutrients. This can be seen as either a plus or a negative and there are pros and cons to both processes. Those with a delicate digestive system who find it hard to process fibre will benefit more from juicing. Also, those who are looking for a fast nutritional 'blast' of vitamins and minerals hitting the system for an instant energy boost. However, this sudden 'juice rush' can cause a spike in blood sugar levels, leading to

mood swings and possible sugar cravings, so it is best to limit the amount of high-sugar fruits in any juice mix to help avoid this. These include the super-sweet fruits such as pineapples, apples, melons, grapes, etc., which should always be mixed with vegetables, especially anything green which does not contain as many natural sugars.

The fibre that is removed in the juicing process can help fill us up, so it is especially useful in weight-loss regimes. Those wishing to include fibre-rich smoothie-style juices in their daily diet can stir some of the juiced pulp back into their glass, or add freshly squeezed juices to high-fibre recipes such as muesli, vegetable soup, and the like. Or they can turn their fresh juice into a smoothie-style drink with the addition of wheatgerm, oatbran, plain yogurt, banana or other lightly bulking ingredients.

Juice power

Because we release more nutrients from fresh fruit and vegetables once they are juiced, we obtain greater levels of nutrition from fresh juices than eating raw fruits and vegetables. We rarely eat a kilo of kale in one sitting, but we might well drink the juice that 1 kilo of kale creates in a single glass. The various organic acids in juices have the ability to scour away waste and harmful bacteria from cells, which means they can deep-cleanse the internal system. For example, pineapples contain citric and malic acids, whilst grapes are rich in tartaric acid, which inhibits the growth of some harmful moulds and bacteria (useful

in wine making). Malic acid is found in apples, apricots, peaches, prunes, plums and lemons (alongside citric acid) as well as many other fruits. It is an excellent natural antiseptic and helps to cleanse the intestines, kidneys, liver and stomach. Citric acid, probably the best-known fruit acid, is found in the highest quantities in citrus fruits and pineapple, and is one of the strongest acid cleansers. Although fruit acids are usually the most commonly talked about, some vegetables also contain beneficial acids, such as lipoic acid, a useful antioxidant found in green leafy vegetables such as broccoli, spinach and other greens. Because juices are such efficient cleansers, naturopaths have used them for decades to help cleanse and restore sick bodies back to health. As part of a daily regime, fresh juices can help keep our system working efficiently and free from waste, making it much harder for unwelcome conditions such as cellulite to take hold.

Your daily detox

It is the cleansing ability of fresh fruit and vegetable juices that makes them a must for all detoxification diets. Some are more aggressive in their cleansing action than others, but as a rough guide, juices from vegetables and sprouted seeds and beans are mild cleansers, whereas fruit juices are strong internal cleansers.

As if all the many health and beauty benefits outlined here are not enough to convince, freshly made juices are virtually fat-free and generally low in calories, making them a valuable part of any weight-loss regime. They also help curb those hunger pangs because the vital nutrients they contain are quickly absorbed into the system, helping to maintain a sense of fullness and satiety. Just be sure to focus more on the vegetable juices rather than the fruit juices (which are naturally higher in sugars).

Ten Good Reasons to Juice

1

Juices are rich
in active enzymes
to aid digestion

2

Juices are packed
with essential vitamins
and minerals

3

Juices help eliminate toxins
and boost our vitality

4

Juices help clear the
complexion and give skin
a radiant healthy glow

5

Juices contain essential
amino acids

6

Juices are rich in the
superfood chlorophyll

7

Juices help balance the
body's acid/alkaline levels

8

Juices are rich in antioxidants
that protect us from disease
and premature ageing

9

Juices help with
weight reduction

10

Fresh juice tastes great!

How we digest our food – and why juicing helps

Without enzymes we cannot digest our food properly and this factor alone makes them vital to health. Enzymes are catalysts, which means they assist in chemical reactions. You could think of them as a highly efficient labour force, constantly breaking down and rebuilding bits of the body. At any one time, millions of enzymes metabolise our food and renew our cells. Without them, the human body would be lifeless. A lack of enzymes means that we cannot convert our food into energy or transform carbohydrates, proteins, fats, vitamins and minerals into muscle, bone, hair, organs, skin and so on. Enzyme deficiency leads to a grave situation where we are literally starving in the midst of plenty because we cannot get what we need from our food.

When our natural enzyme level gets low, our metabolism slows, we get tired and all our bodily functions begin to suffer. Cells are not repaired and renewed efficiently, which means we age more quickly. The more we can conserve our own natural enzymes by eating food that is raw and 'alive', the healthier we will be and the longer – and stronger – we are likely to live. Eating raw foods – in this case using raw fruit and vegetables for juicing – is the best way to replenish and preserve enzymes within the body.

If we consider what is actually involved in digesting food from beginning to end we can start to appreciate just how much energy it takes to do this. Food travels through over 9 metres of digestive tubing (the gastrointestinal tract), passing through both the large and small intestine. Although tightly folded within us, if unfurled at microscopic level this would produce a total surface area large enough to cover an entire tennis court (and that's just for one individual). The amount of energy it takes to digest food through this lengthy and complex system is called the Thermic Effect of Food (TEF). This is the amount of energy needed to process the foods we eat over and above our normal resting metabolic rate (i.e. when we are still and not using energy for other activities). Generally speaking, our TEF is around 10 per cent, i.e. it takes 10 per cent of the calories in the food we eat to process it through the body. Dietary fat, such as butter and oils, are very easy to process (around 5 per cent TEF) and have very little thermic effect, whereas the protein in meat is harder to digest and has a higher TEF of around 15 per cent. The reason why many of us can feel tired after a large meal is because the body is forced to divert more of its energy for digestion. Juicing can help here because it increases the supply of live enzymes to boost the digestive process, lower TEF and leave more energy for other bodily functions, such as fighting disease and detoxification. If all the body's available energy is used for digestion it may not be able to eliminate toxins properly, which can then lead to a range of health problems – from cellulite to cancer.

This underpins the thinking of leading health and beauty experts who advocate fresh juice fasts as a way of conserving the body's energy for cleansing and renewal. Interestingly, it has been widely reported that eating raw celery or grapefruit has a negative caloric balance as it takes more energy to digest them then is converted into calories – but this theory, whilst quite possibly true, has yet to be proven.

Many enzymes require the presence of other nutrients, such as vitamins and minerals, before a chemical reaction can take place. These nutrients are known as co-factors. Raw food provides us with the complete package of enzymes and co-factors needed to break down that particular food and release its valuable nutrients for vitality.

Enzymes are sensitive to heat and are destroyed by high temperatures. They can also be damaged by exposure to air and by freezing. Essentially, the food many of us eat is 'dead' because the active component has been destroyed by various manufacturing processes. Freshly squeezed juices give us live enzymes, complete with their co-factors – exactly what we need to be properly nourished.

Juicing nutrition

Generally, vitamins fall into two groups – the water-soluble ones that include B vitamins and vitamin C, and the fat-soluble ones that include vitamins A, D, E and K. The body can store fat-soluble vitamins for a limited amount of time, but water-soluble ones, apart from vitamin B12, need to be constantly topped-up through the food and drink we consume. Like enzymes, vitamins are essential to life; if we became completely deficient in one or more vitamins, we would eventually expire. Don't panic though – in most cases vitamin deficiencies are easy to spot. Vitamins are widely available in many foods and if we eat a well-balanced diet we can be reasonably sure of getting the right amounts.

Vitamins have an amazing impact on our health. Without adequate supplies, enzyme efficiency is decreased, and we can fall prey to a host of vitamin-deficiency diseases, such as rickets, beriberi, scurvy and reproductive abnormalities.

Individual vitamin requirements vary from person to person and according to our stage of life. For most of us, the recommended daily allowances (RDAs, see opposite) are a reasonably good guide to how much we need; however, some of us may need far more than this, for example pregnant or breastfeeding women, the elderly, infants and young children, and people who follow particular diets such as vegetarians and vegans.

A number of other factors affect our vitamin status, for example inadequate diet, impaired digestion, overcooking, food processing, bad storage of food and irradiation. Added to these are lifestyle factors such as smoking and excessive alcohol, which can further rob the body of these valuable nutrients. Fresh juices provide one of the best ways of ensuring we are consuming adequate supplies of vitamins in a balanced form together with their mineral counter parts.

Minerals matter

Like vitamins, minerals are essential to good health; many of us are familiar with the relationship between zinc and healthy skin and between iron and healthy blood. Minerals divide into two groups – major minerals and minor or trace minerals. The major group includes calcium, magnesium, sodium, potassium, phosphorus, sulphur and chlorine. The minor or trace minerals include zinc, iron, chromium, copper, fluorine, silicon, iodine, manganese, selenium, nickel, tin, vanadium, molybdenum, cobalt – and even arsenic! Although we only need tiny amounts of these minor minerals they are all absolutely essential to our good health and vitality. Overall, this complex of major and minor minerals gives nutritional quality to our food and there is no greater natural source than fresh fruit and vegetables. Together, all vitamins and minerals combine to form a nutritional group known as micronutrients, so-called because they are needed in only very small amounts – but even in these tiny quantities they are essential.

There are generally agreed Recommended Daily Allowances – known as RDAs – for the important vitamins and minerals. However, many nutritionists believe that these RDA figures represent, at best, a *minimum* daily allowance because commercially grown foods have, in many cases, lost substantial nutritional value. The nutrition scientist Dr Linus Pauling, recipient of two Nobel Prizes, stated that 'Doctors claim that the ordinary diet will give you all the vitamins you need – this is not true – we do not get the amounts needed in the average diet, which does not contain all the nutrients we need for good health'. The author of *A Time to Heal*, Beata Bishop, who was given six months to live in 1981, always claimed she won her battle against cancer by following the Gerson Therapy diet (see page 32). She believes the average Western diet to be inadequate, declaring that 'not only is our appearance at stake, but the fundamentals of good health are at risk'.

In order to stay healthy we really need to make sure that we get *at least* the RDA of the important minerals and vitamins, and making raw juices part of our daily intake can help us do this swiftly and easily. The vitamin and mineral charts on the following pages show the RDAs and uses of the essential vitamins, as well as good food sources for each.

Vitamin / RDA	Essential for	Good sources for juicers
Vitamin A 0.7mg men 0.6mg women	Growth; healthy skin, lungs, eyes and eyesight; helps to fight infection	Yellow, orange, red and dark green fruit and vegetables, notably dandelion greens, carrots, broccoli, kale, spinach, cantaloupe melon, apricot and tomatoes
Vitamin E 4mg men 3mg women	Reproduction; protects against heart disease; acts as an antioxidant and protects all cell membranes	Cabbage, Brussels sprouts, green leafy vegetables – including spinach, beet greens and dandelion greens, sprouted seeds and beans, avocados
Vitamin K 0.001mg a day per kilo of body weight (e.g. 70kg needs 0.07mg a day)	Blood clotting, helping with wound healing	Green leafy vegetables, including broccoli, kale and spinach, asparagus
Vitamin B complex *(made up of many B vitamins, each with their own RDA – see below)*	Healthy nervous system; carbohydrate, protein and fat metabolism; healthy hair, skin and eyes; red blood-cell formation; proper liver function	Green leafy vegetables, citrus fruit, strawberries
B1 Thiamin 1mg men 0.8mg women	Works with other B vitamins to release energy from food; keeps nerves and muscles healthy	Cauliflower, peas, asparagus, kale, potatoes, oranges
B2 Riboflavin 1.3mg men 1.1mg women	Healthy skin, eyes and nervous system; releases energy from carbohydrates	Asparagus, bananas, persimmons, okra, Swiss chard, green beans, leafy green vegetables, tomatoes

Vitamin / RDA	Essential for	Good sources for juicers
B3 Niacin 17mg men 13mg women	Produces energy from food; keeps nervous and digestive systems healthy	Avocados, tomatoes, green leafy vegetables, broccoli, carrots, sweet potatoes, asparagus
Vitamin B6 (pyridoxine) 1.4mg men 1.2mg women	Helps the body produce and store energy; carries oxygen throughout the system	Prunes, potatoes, bananas, chilli, green beans, tomatoes, spinach
Folic Acid (vitamin B9) 0.2mg adults 0.4mg in early stages of pregnancy	Works with vitamin B12 to create healthy blood cells; helps prevent central nervous system damage in unborn babies (in first 12 weeks of life)	Green leafy vegetables – notably spinach, green beans, peas, broccoli, kale, beet greens, dandelion greens, asparagus
Vitamin B12 (cobalamin) 0.0015mg adults	Helps produce red blood cells and keeps nervous system healthy; works with folic acid; helps release energy from food	Chlorella and other freshwater algae
Bioflavonoids (no known RDA)	Works alongside vitamin C as an antioxidant; helps increase capillary strength and reduce inflammation in cells	Citrus fruits, blackcurrants, blueberries, parsley
Vitamin C 40mg adults	Immune system; wound healing; fighting infection; healthy bones and teeth; guards against stress; an antioxidant	Citrus fruits, broccoli, potatoes, red peppers, tomatoes, strawberries, blackcurrants,

UK Department of Health 2014

mg – milligrams

Mineral / RDA	Essential for	Good sources for juicers
Calcium 700mg adults	Strong, healthy bones and teeth; muscle action; nerve function; normal blood clotting and heart function	Dark green leaves, especially kale and turnip tops, broccoli, cabbage and okra (but not spinach) and dandelion greens
Iodine 0.14mg adults	Production of thyroxine which regulates metabolism and energy production, needed for physical and mental development	Green leafy vegetables, cabbage, pineapple, strawberries and plants grown on iodine-rich soil
Chromium 0.025mg adults	Helps regulate insulin and control blood sugars; boosts vitality by releasing energy from food	Broccoli, asparagus, green beans, prunes, potatoes, bananas
Iron 8.7mg men 14.8mg women	Healthy blood, haemoglobin production, oxygenating the blood; promotes growth	Green leafy vegetables – notably spinach, Swiss chard, kale and beet greens, apricots, prunes, parsley
Magnesium 300mg men 270mg women	Healthy bones and muscles (works with calcium); helps control blood sugars	Dark green vegetables, especially kale and spinach
Phosphorus 550mg adults	Builds and maintains bones and teeth, nervous tissue and hair; helps with absorption of fats and carbohydrates	Asparagus, carrots, endive, kale, parsnips, spinach, watercress
Potassium 3500mg adults	Muscle contraction; nerve transmission; healthy skin; water balance (works with sodium); lowers blood pressure	Most vegetables and fruit, notably bananas
Selenium 0.075mg men 0.06mg women	Antioxidant, plays an important role in both the immune system and fertility	Broccoli, tomatoes
Sodium No more than 2.4g daily is recommended (average UK intake is 3.7mg)	Muscle contraction; nerve transmission; fluid balance; aids digestion by balancing digestive fluids	Carrots, endive, parsley
Zinc 5.5–9.5mg men 4.7mg women	Helps create new cells and enzymes, speeds wound healing	Sea vegetables, e.g. chlorella, alfalfa, blackcurrants

Mineral deficiency

Although vitamin deficiencies can be corrected fairly quickly, the same isn't true for minerals. We can build up long-term deficiencies where the effects are gradual and insidious. A chromium deficiency, for example, may show up as bouts of fatigue, exhaustion and hunger. Magnesium deficiency can lead to premenstrual tension (PMT), depression, muscle tremors and disorientation. Zinc deficiency can lead to infertility. Iron deficiency, one of the most prevalent mineral deficiencies, affects one-fifth of the world's population. It is very common in menstruating women who lose iron every month. Symptoms include anaemia, brittle nails, weakness, fatigue and breathing impairment. Vegetarian and vegan diets sometimes contain insufficient iron, since red meat is such a good source.

Correcting mineral deficiencies takes much longer than correcting vitamin deficiencies, so it is essential that we always meet our daily requirements. Juices can help you achieve this, while at the same time improving your skin, hair, nails – and moods! See opposite for the RDAs and uses of the essential minerals, together with good food sources that can be juiced.

How amino acids help

Fresh fruit and vegetables enrich the diet with amino acids in an easily digestible form. Amino acids are the building blocks of protein. They work hand in hand with enzymes and are responsible for an array of diverse functions, from making hormones and blood to building muscles and organs. One of their key functions is the digestion and assimilation of food, and if this doesn't happen, other bodily functions begin to suffer. A deficiency of amino acids can trigger a range of symptoms from digestive disorders and allergies to premature ageing. A daily dose of essential amino acids from drinking raw fruit and vegetable juices can really make a difference to your health, and juices made from leafy greens and sprouts are especially rich in amino acids. Some of the most commonly available are alanine (found in carrots, green leafy vegetables and beetroot), cysteine (found in beetroot, cabbage, apples and pineapple) and lysine (found in carrots, cucumber, celery and spinach).

The importance of chlorophyll

Chlorophyll, the molecule that gives plants their green colour, is the stuff that enables all plants to photosynthesise – the process of converting sunlight, water and carbon dioxide into glucose, the food of plants, without which they wouldn't be able to grow. Chlorophyll stands at the base of all food chains because all living creatures on the planet – including humans – obtain their energy supply from plants.

Chlorophyll is rated extremely highly by naturopaths and dieticians because it cleanses the system, builds the blood and cells and makes a wonderful all-round regenerative tonic. (How many of us could survive without the occasional tonic?) One of the best ways to introduce high amounts of chlorophyll into your diet is by drinking green juices, in particular alfalfa, wheat grass (see pages 77–78), leafy greens, watercress, green peppers, celery and cucumbers.

The power of antioxidants

Antioxidants have long been hailed as the secret to living longer and looking younger. The three principal antioxidant nutrients found in fruits and vegetables used for juicing are vitamin A (or, more accurately, its vegetable precursor beta-carotene), vitamin C and vitamin E. Each has a protective effect on the other, which means that their combined power is greater than any of them singly. There are many other more recently highlighted antioxidants to be found in fresh fruit and vegetables, such as the anthocyanins (the nutritious red, yellow and purple pigments that give so many plants their colourful hue).

Since my first book on the potent powers of antioxidants in the diet was published back in 1995, much medical evidence has shown that antioxidants can help prevent cancer, cardiovascular disease and other chronic, degenerative diseases – even slowing the ageing process. There have been hundreds of world-class clinical studies into the extraordinary powers of these incredible nutrients, many of which have produced impressive results.

So how do they work?

Antioxidants mop up the baddies in the body, which are called free radicals. They form as a result of normal bodily function, but in excess they cause problems. To understand why free radicals are so damaging, we need to know how they work. Essentially, they are highly unstable electrons that react with and damage other molecules; these damaged molecules have been linked to almost every degenerative disease, from cell destruction and enzyme damage to growth of cancer tumours. In fact, research in this area suggests that free radicals are a major contributor to at least 50 of the most prevalent diseases – including heart and lung disease, certain cancers, cataracts, rheumatoid arthritis – as well as the ageing process.

We can see the damaging effects of free radicals by observing a freshly sliced apple turn brown. This happens when the cut surface of the apple comes into contact with the air and begins to oxidise. However, a squeeze of lemon juice on the apple protects it from damage because the vitamin C in the lemon juice acts as an antioxidant. Kitchen chemistry!

How can we protect ourselves?

As antioxidants are the key to protection against free-radical damage, we want to keep our intake of antioxidants high while at the same time avoiding the things that encourage the formation of free radicals, such as pollution, smoking, barbecued and blackened foods, foods fried in oil, ultraviolet radiation (including excess sunshine) and alcohol. Drinking fresh juices ensures we get enough antioxidants in our daily diet to help fight the free-radical damage going on inside the body: the Gerson Therapy diet includes ten fresh fruit and vegetable juices every day to protect against general disease.

Vitamin A as an antioxidant

There are two types of vitamin A: retinol, which is generally found in animal foods, especially organ meats such as liver; and beta-carotene, found in fruit and vegetables. High doses of retinol can be toxic, whereas beta-carotene is considered safe in any amounts. Beta-carotene is easily converted into retinol within the body and therefore adequate supplies of beta-carotene should provide enough retinol. Excess beta-carotene is then available to be used as an antioxidant. The ability of vitamin A to scavenge free-radicals is strongest in the lining of the tissues within the body, and it has been shown to help prevent cancer formation. This vitamin is also vital in protecting the thymus gland, one of the immune system's most important organs. Beta-carotene is found in all fruit and vegetables and is especially high in yellow and orange fruit and vegetables and in dark green leaves. So go for colourful abundance in your shopping basket.

Vitamin C as an antioxidant

Citrus fruits, potatoes, green leaves and tomatoes are all great sources of vitamin C, which is one of the most protective substances we have. It strengthens the immune system and helps to fight infections and heal wounds. Vitamin C is also found bound with other micronutrients, such as bioflavonoids, which also have antioxidant and anti-inflammatory properties. For example, one bioflavonoid, rutin, is found in the pith of citrus fruits and can help strengthen and protect skin cells. For this reason alone it's worth eating the pith and inner skins of oranges and grapefruits – or at least making sure they get added to the juicer. Being water-soluble, vitamin C is not stored in the body but is excreted daily in our sweat and urine so it is important to have a good daily supply.

Vitamin E as an antioxidant

Vitamin E can help protect the body against the toxic effects of damaged fats – (i.e. when a fat is artificially hardened, such as hydrogenated palm oil, or overheated, in the case of deep-fat fryers. Vitamin E is particularly effective in helping to protect against wrinkled skin tissues and damage to cells, including damage caused by smoking. Although this fat-soluble vitamin mostly occurs in plant oils, nuts and seeds, it can also be found in avocado, asparagus and green vegetables, especially watercress. Many of the foods rich in vitamin E are expensive and seasonal, so adding the contents of a pierced vitamin E capsule to your juice recipe is an easy and economical way of ensuring you get an adequate year-round supply.

Micro-antioxidants

Other nutrients on the antioxidant team are the trace mineral selenium and the amino acid cysteine, both found in fruit and vegetables. Spinach, broccoli, peas and tomatoes are sources of selenium and beetroot, carrots, cabbage, kale, apple, pineapple and raspberries all provide cysteine. Selenium works well with vitamin E and they are often hailed as the anti-ageing nutritional duo. Selenium's protective functions have also been found to lessen the risk of heart disease and cancer – two life-threatening conditions that are far more prevalent in areas of the world with low levels of selenium in the soil. Intensive modern farming practices that rely on synthetic chemicals deplete levels of selenium from the soil – just one reason why fruit and vegetables should be grown organically or in non-chemically treated soil with naturally high levels of selenium.

Vitality

When was the last time you felt really vibrant, ready to run a mile or climb a mountain? ... Really? That long?!

In order to have high vitality we need to eat high-vitality foods. This means eating foods that are alive (i.e. raw) and packed with active enzymes, vitamins, minerals and other essential nutrients. As a rule of thumb, the fresher the food, the more vitality it contains. Many of us may have forgotten what true vitality feels like as we have become increasingly accustomed to a diet that contains too much processed food and a sedentary lifestyle, both of which encourage a lack of energy.

On a vitality scale of one to ten, raw foods and juices come at the top, while processed and tinned foods sit at the bottom. Juices made with raw ingredients are fantastic energy boosters. They are rapidly digested in the stomach and absorbed into the bloodstream more quickly than eating unjuiced fruit and veggies. This makes their journey round the body, nourishing and revitalising the cells, a speedy and efficient process.

How juices help heal

Back in the 1940s a German-born American physician, Dr Max Gerson, developed a non-toxic approach to treating chronic diseases, including cancer, and his daughter went on to found the Gerson Institute in San Diego, California. Gerson discovered that his patients tended to recover from degenerative illness when put on a diet made up largely of fresh raw juices. After years of dietary experiments, he designed the stringent Gerson Therapy programme, which includes drinking ten fresh juices a day. Going against the grain of medical wisdom, he claimed to be able to cure cancer by diet alone when all other treatments had failed. A bold claim, but one that gained him many followers, some of which have indeed gone into remission after following his extreme juicing treatment plan.

We can measure the vitamins, minerals and other elements that plants contain, such as flavours and so on, but there is another, less easily measured component to plants that aids in the healing process. It is this intangible or subtle energy that many natural health practitioners are convinced helps provide the life spark in all living organisms. The more raw food we eat, the more of this life energy we receive. This is why raw fruit and vegetable juice can help us rediscover the energy we once had and the health we thought we had lost, as well as giving us the radiant glow of a healthy properly functioning body. Vibrant health not only makes us feel intoxicated with life but also it gives us the drive to fulfil our goals. Yes!!

Why balancing acid and alkaline matters

A diet that includes fruit and vegetable juices helps us to maintain and restore the correct acid/alkaline balance in the body. In a strange paradox, most organic acids foods have an alkalising effect on the body, whereas alkaline foods have an acid effect on the body. Therefore, if we eat acidic foods, the ultimate effect on the body is alkalising! Strange but true. The so-called Alkaline Diet, which has been so fashionable amongst Hollywood celebrities, is simply one based on eating plenty of (alkalising) fresh fruits and vegetables and minimising the intake of (acid-forming) sugar, alcohol and processed foods. Following a juice-rich diet can help increase the alkalinity of your daily food intake, especially if you focus more on vegetable juices that are lower in natural sugars.

Many chronic medical conditions are exacerbated by high acidity and many of us in the 'developed world' eat far too much in the way of acid-forming foods, such as sugar, meat and processed foods. These can all unbalance the body's natural acid/alkaline balance, which can in turn lead to various health problems including arthritis, gout and fatigue. Added to that, lifestyle factors such as stress, overwork and other modern malaises further increase the acid load. A typical Western diet, high in animal proteins, refined sugar and flour, synthetic additives and chemical prescription drugs, causes acids to build up in our cells. Acid cells are believed to attract toxins and waste matter, which in turn may make the cells more acidic. It's known that cancer cells flourish in an acid environment, so it is sensible to avoid a build-up of acids within the system.

How to achieve the best acid/alkaline balance

You've guessed it – eat more fruit and vegetables! In this respect juices really do come into their own, because you are using every bit of the plant, and they provide a delicious way to keep the balance right. In general fruit, especially citrus, comes out top in its alkalising effects on the body.

Power-packed with nutrients, with an ability to help re-balance the body, restore vitality, get the skin glowing *and* shed a few kilos in the process, there's no time like Now! to develop a healthy love of juicing.

– 2 –

Getting started

Equipment

The first thing you need, if you don't already have one, is a juicer, ideally one of the high-speed electric juicers. These not only work for citrus fruits but can also extract juice from hard fruit and vegetables such as carrots, beetroot, apples and potatoes. It is definitely worth checking whether the juicer can be washed in a dishwasher (they can be fiddly to clean) since high dishwasher temperatures could warp some plastic parts.

The juicer market has exploded in recent years and there are very many different types and models of electric juicing machines to choose from. Juicers generally fall into three categories:

- **Citrus presses**, which, as their name suggests, essentially only press oranges, grapefruits, lemons etc. They are not suitable for juicing the whole fruit.

- **Centrifugal juicers**, which work by means of a rapidly spinning blade and centrifugal force whizzing around a central cavity, forcing pulp one way and juice the other. Most kitchen appliance brands have their own versions (some brands make several different varieties). The main differences tend to be the power of the motor. The more powerful the machine, the faster it will juice. The more powerful machines may also be slightly better built, as they need a sturdier housing for the motor. They can be a good investment if you're intending to juice on a daily basis, as being more robust, they tend to have a longer working

Now that we know why fresh juices are so enriching for health, beauty and added vitality, it's time to get started. A well-thought-out juicing programme can be the first step towards a fresh, revitalising health regime and a Brand New You!

life. Much has been written about the benefits of 'slow juicers' which – as their name suggests – crush fruit and veg in a slower way, more akin to a cold-pressing action. The theory is that this preserves nutritional values by avoiding excess heat in the rotor blades, but research has shown that high-speed juicers are more efficient at extracting the juice (and therefore higher levels of nutrients) so may be a better option. My personal favourite juicing machine is one with a high-powered motor and wide 'feeding tube' to accommodate whole apples and larger pieces of veg – which also saves time chopping!

- **Masticating juicers**, these have more of a grinding action, are slower but can also be more efficient (they extract about a third more juice than some centrifugal juicers). Masticating juicers can juice a wider variety of produce, including herbs and plants (such as wheat grass), nuts and seeds. It's claimed that they crush juices using far less heat, thereby reducing oxidation (so your juice will last longer) but are also highly efficient, so retain more nutritional value. However they are much more expensive and not an essential piece of everyday kitchen kit.

Sourcing your fruit and vegetables

Having bought your juicer, the next essential step is to establish a good, plentiful and inexpensive source of fresh fruit and vegetables. It's worth scouting around your local area to see what's available – you may have a farmers' market nearby, or be able to organise a weekly veg box delivery. Local greengrocers are a good option and may offer bulk discounts for regular customers, or reduced prices just before closing time (supermarkets do this too). You may even be lucky enough to pick up bags of free farm produce that is too misshapen to be sold in the shops – search online or see pages 188–189.

To be sure of the quality of the fruit and veg they should be organic or grown without the use of toxic fertilisers or pesticides. This is especially important when juicing produce in their skins (such as apples, carrots, etc.). If juicing skins-and-all, scrub first with a brush in warm, soapy water, then rinse well and pat dry before juicing. This will remove most of the sprayed-on chemical residues, such as post-harvest fungicides. I also wash the skins of fruits that are to be peeled, such as oranges, as traces can linger on knives and chopping boards. When in doubt – wash! Organically grown crops are free from harmful chemicals and benefit from higher levels of nutrients, such as antioxidants. Intensively farmed crops are grown in soils depleted by aggressive farming methods. Artificial fertilisers can cause minerals such as calcium, magnesium and selenium to be so diluted in the soil that they are not taken up by the plants. Pesticides can accumulate in our bodies, affecting our digestion and interfering with nutrient absorption. Although all pesticides are thoroughly tested, many were originally approved when standards were comparatively lax. In addition, pesticides are tested individually and no one knows what the long-term effects are of ingesting a daily cocktail of these chemicals. It may come as a surprise to learn that, despite the health warnings, the use of pesticides has steadily increased over the years. Alarmingly, pesticide residues in fruit and vegetables almost doubled in the UK between 2003 and 2013. Almost half of our food contains toxic pesticide residues and some residues found in fruit and veg exceed the permitted limits. The highest levels are found in soft citrus fruits, such as tangerines and satsumas. The most recent study published in the UK (2011), at the time of writing, showed that all samples tested contained pesticide residues, with 96 per cent containing residues of more than one pesticide. That study revealed soft citrus, oranges, pineapple and grapes all had pesticides at levels exceeding the UK government's permitted MRLs (Maximum Residue Levels). So at the very least it is worth ensuring that these fruits are sourced organically.

Pesticides

The produce most likely to contain pesticide residues are (in order): soft citrus, oranges, pears, pineapple, grapes, apples, raspberries, carrots, spinach, pre-packed salads and peppers. Carbendazim, a pesticide linked to birth defects, is the most commonly applied pesticide – and it's used on a lot of the produce we are most likely to put through a juicer: oranges, apples, cucumber, pineapple, pre-packed salads, raspberries, soft citrus and spinach. Chlorpyrifos residue was found on over half of all oranges tested. This pesticide was recently made infamous because it has been shown to harm honey bees. Chlorpyrifos has also been found on apples, grapes, pears and spinach. Cypermethrin, a pesticide found in courgettes, grapes, soft citrus and spinach, is another hazardous chemical listed by the EU Environmental Protection Agency (EPA) as a likely carcinogen, as well as being considered highly toxic to bees. Similarly, the pesticide Dieldrin has been found in courgettes and cucumbers, despite being a known endocrine disruptor, which means that it can affect the hormones, resulting in tumours and birth and developmental defects. (It is worth noting that 38 per cent of all samples found were from produce grown in the UK.)

Possibly one of the most controversial pesticide residues currently on the increase is Glyphosate, also known as Roundup and sold by the American biotechnology company Monsanto as it is required to grow GM-crops. Unfortunately, GM-plants are demanding ever greater applications of Roundup to control the super-weeds around GM-crops, which inevitably result in higher levels of residues being present in our food. Other insecticides that keen juicers should be made aware of are Methomyl, a thyroid-disrupting chemical that has been detected in celery (another favourite ingredient for juicing), and Lambda-cyhalothrin, a pesticide also found in celery, as well as pre-packed salads and spinach.

The real issue here is not individual traces of these toxic chemicals commonly found on intensively farmed fruit and veg, most of which are well within government agency 'permitted levels', but the cumulative 'cocktail' effect of ingesting dozens of these residues in a single sitting. Since no one can know the impact of this on our health, it is worth ensuring that the majority of your juicing materials are grown organically or home-grown without using pesticides. (See Useful Addresses for more information on buying chemical-free ingredients, page 188.)

Go organic!

By contrast, organically grown fruits and vegetables are free of traces of artificial fertilisers and pesticides. They contain higher levels of some vitamins, minerals and micronutrients, they're far better for the environment, far better for soil fertility – and far better for us. And in my opinion (and many others) they simply taste better!

The Soil Association is an excellent resource for providing details of certified organic farmers, growers and suppliers in your area (see Useful Addresses, page 188) including home-delivery schemes. However, if you find it impossible to get hold of a particular ingredient that has been grown organically, there are a few steps you can take to choose the next best option. One is to buy locally grown. No guarantee over pesticide residues, but local, seasonal produce is more likely to be grown in more natural environmental conditions (unlike intensively cultivated, unseasonal crops shipped around the globe). At least this way, if you can't avoid the possible agrichemical residues, you can ensure the nutrient content hasn't been depleted by early harvesting, artificial gas-ripening or lengthy cold storage. The longer a fruit or vegetable is transported, artificially ripened or stored, the faster it deteriorates. Produce from abroad is often picked well before it ripens, which means it has less time to gather essential nutrients from the sun and soil. Buying locally grown fruit and vegetables in season also helps us keep in touch with the ebb and flow of nature's cycle and ensures we get the nutrients we need, when we need them. Don't be afraid to question your local supplier or supermarket about where their produce comes from and what chemicals have been used in its supply. Local greengrocers normally have a good idea of where their fruit and vegetables are grown – and might even be persuaded to stock organic and locally grown produce. Ideally, grow as much of your own as you can – from a full kitchen garden to a small tub of tomatoes or a window box of spinach. There's always room for something – even if it's just herbs in pots on a windowsill, a tray of wheat grass, beansprouts or alfalfa sprouts germinated on dampened kitchen paper – for the ultimate in fresh, tasty juices.

Remember:

- The fresher the fruit and vegetables, the richer they are in nutrients.

- Organic has to be healthier as the fewer harmful chemicals used, the better for you the produce is likely to be.

Shopping tips:

- Buy organic produce whenever possible.

- Buy local produce that is in season.

- Shop frequently to ensure fresh and ripe produce – and avoid waste.

- Share a bulk-buy box scheme with a juicing friend to keep costs down.

- Keep fruit and vegetables stored in a cool, dry place so they last longer.

My favourite fruit and vegetables

The following pages describe forty of the most commonly juiced ingredients, with a guide to their health and healing powers. Generally speaking, fruits are considered to be a better source of vitamins than vegetables, whereas vegetables are considered to be the better source of minerals. (Check the nutrient composition tables (see pages 22–24) for details of the individual fruits and vegetables listed here.) Fruits are highly eliminative, meaning they are good at getting rid of waste and toxins within the body, especially citrus fruits, pineapples and grapes; vegetables have a milder cleansing action on the body and are extremely restorative, meaning they provide high levels of energy in an easily digestible way.

Unjuiceables

A very few fruit and vegetables do not lend themselves to juicing, mainly because it is hard to extract the juice from their pulp. Avocados, bananas and coconuts fall into this category. Rhubarb is also

best left alone because it contains a high amount of oxalic acid (which interferes with the absorbtion of certain minerals in the body) and has an overly sharp, bitter taste.

Actinidia deliciosa KIWI FRUIT

This strange-looking little fruit used to be known as a 'Chinese gooseberry' until New Zealand growers changed the name to 'kiwi fruit' to make it more marketable. In health terms, kiwi fruits are a great source of vitamin C, containing twice as much per gram as oranges. They are also rich in vitamins E and K, beta-carotene, potassium and omega-3 essential fatty acids, all of which can help reduce high blood pressure. They are excellent for general cleansing and helping to ward off colds and 'flu. The flavour of kiwi juice has been compared to a mixture of pineapple and strawberries – and it certainly helps perk up weaker-tasting juices.

Buying and preparing:
Kiwi fruit should be firm but not hard, yielding to slight pressure. As with all hot-weather and tropical fruits, kiwis are imported and available all year round and can be stored for quite a while in the fridge. They are one of the few fruits that should really be peeled before juicing (or very well-scrubbed).

Juice rating:
114–170ml per 450g of kiwi fruit

Ananas comosus PINEAPPLE

Pineapples are native to tropical America, and were highly rated among the discoveries of Columbus. Nowadays, they are also grown in other parts of the world (notably Kenya) and are available throughout the year.

Because of their high vitamin C content, pineapples are considered to be a protective fruit as vitamin C is so important for our immune system. Other nutrients found in pineapples include beta-carotene, folic acid, potassium, iodine, calcium, magnesium and manganese.

Pineapple juice is wonderful for relieving constipation and poor digestion and the combination of vitamin C, fruit acids and enzymes makes pineapples highly eliminative and a great boost for detox diets. In particular, one of the digestive enzymes pineapple contains – bromelain – is amazingly efficient at breaking down protein and dissolving excess mucus; so effective, in fact, that workers in canning factories have to wear protective gloves to stop their skin from being eaten away by the juice. Bromelain also balances the body's acid/alkaline levels, soothes sore throats and has been found to help cases of laryngitis.

Buying and preparing:
Pineapples should have a golden-coloured skin and smell strong and sweet. The best test of ripeness is whether you can pull a leaf off the stem easily – if not, then it is not ripe. Before juicing, remove the spiny top and peel. You can juice the flesh and the core. Pineapples should be stored at room temperature when whole or in an airtight container in the fridge if cut into pieces.

Juice rating:
114–170ml per 450g of pineapple

Apium graveolens CELERY

Celery has long been regarded for its healing powers. In ancient times it was used in the Far East to cure stomach complaints and as a general tonic. The Greeks prized celery so highly they even awarded it to their winning sportsmen. Celery seeds were once used as painkillers, while chemicals in the sticks have been shown to lower blood pressure. Drinking the juice can help soothe digestive ailments and counteract acidosis (an excess of acid in the body's fluids). It is also reputed to help balance blood pH levels, preventing the build-up of acid in the joints, which contributes to arthritis.

Celery also contains interesting concentrations of essential oils, which account for its distinctive smell. These oils are thought to have a beneficial effect on our digestive system. Celery leaves can be juiced too, along with the roots if you're pulling it from the kitchen garden.

Celery provides a useful source of potassium, sodium and sulphur. A combination of celery and apple juice is reputed to be an excellent blood and body purifier for those living in polluted urban areas. As an added bonus to celery's health-giving virtues, it is also reputed to boost a flagging sex drive...!

Buying and preparing:
Celery sticks should be firm and crisp with fresh-looking leaves. They need to be washed before juicing and can be stored in the fridge. Do include the green leafy tops in your juicing.

Juice rating:
28ml per 2 or 3 celery sticks

Asparagus officinalis ASPARAGUS

Asparagus is a member of the lily family that includes other vegetables such as onions, leeks and garlic. It was popular in Roman times and is another vegetable ingredient thought to have strong aphrodisiac powers. It's a good source of folic acid and vitamin C. Asparagus is a highly alkaline food and so it is considered a good vegetable to include in elimination diets. It is reputed to cleanse the blood and tissues of waste matter and helps to dissolve kidney stones. According to vegetable juicing pioneer the late Norman Walker DSc, asparagus juice helps to break up oxalic acid crystals in the kidneys and muscles, which makes it useful in treating rheumatism. Green-tipped asparagus is high in vitamin A (beta-carotene), which improves hair, skin and eyes, and can guard against cancer. Many of the elements that benefit the liver, kidneys, skin and bones are found in asparagus; they include the vitamins A, B1, C and E, folic acid and potassium.

The raw juice makes a particularly effective diuretic (promoting the production of urine) and mixes well with carrot and cucumber in this respect. Some research suggests that asparagus juice contains enzymes that help break down alcohol; it may be useful as an addition to a hangover tonic. Asparagus contains sulphur compounds that make urine smell sulphurous as quickly as 15–20 minutes after eating.

Buying and preparing:
Look for bright green asparagus with firm, fresh tips. Do not buy spears that are old and woody or limp-looking. Asparagus will keep for a few days in the fridge and should be juiced before it starts to wilt.

Juice rating:
28ml per 3 or 4 asparagus spears

Beta Vulgaris BEETROOT

Beetroot has been cultivated since the fourth century BC and in ancient times was only used for medicinal purposes. Nowadays it is widely enjoyed as a delicious vegetable, while it continues to be valued for its therapeutic properties. Beetroot juice is one of the most powerful cleansers and blood builders. It contains many nutrients including folic acid, magnesium and a highly absorbable form of iron to help build red blood corpuscles. Although the iron content of beetroot is not particularly high, it is of a form that is easily assimilated. Because of this, beetroot juice also has a therapeutic effect on menstrual disturbances and can relieve some of the uncomfortable effects of the menopause. Beetroot juice is reputedly nourishing for the gall bladder, kidneys and liver. Its high beta-carotene content makes it good for both the digestive and lymphatic systems and it helps promote the elimination of toxins. Recent research has shown beetroot to be rich in dietary nitrate, which can help lower blood pressure and improve blood flow. Beetroot also contains betaines, compounds of a red colour that are not broken down by the body, which is why urine and stools turn purplish-red after eating or drinking the juice – a quite disconcerting effect if you are not expecting it! Since beetroot juice is a powerful kidney and blood cleanser you may want to mix it with other juices (apple, carrot, cucumber), which will also soften the powerful taste. The dark green beet tops can be juiced as well, so don't discard as they are packed with beta-carotene and chlorophyll.

Buying and preparing:
Often beetroot is cooked before being sold, but try to buy it raw. Scrub well and remove the toughened stalks (but not the leaves) before juicing.

Juice rating:
170–227ml per 450g of beetroots or leaves

Brassica oleracea BROCCOLI

Broccoli is a member of the cabbage or brassica family and is a real winner when it comes to carotenoids, as it contains high levels of beta-carotene, folic acid and manganese and also the much talked about compound sulforaphane, which may make it a great cancer-preventing super food. The American Cancer Society recommends that we eat broccoli several times a week, which, it claims, 'might reduce the incidence of colon, stomach and oesophageal cancer'. Broccoli is also a rich source of vitamins C, B1 and folic acid and the minerals calcium, sulphur, iron, potassium and selenium. It has similar therapeutic properties to its relatives (cabbage, cauliflower and Brussels sprouts, etc.) and is particularly good for maintaining healthy hair, skin and eyes.

Buying and preparing:
Choose bright green heads with tight tops. Yellow or brown loose heads are past their best. The stems should be firm with fresh-looking leaves; avoid woody stems. Broccoli is available throughout the year, but because it does not keep for long it should be used within a few days. Before juicing, always wash broccoli thoroughly.

Juice rating:
114–142ml per 450g of broccoli

Brassica oleracea CABBAGE

Cabbage (another brassica, along with kale, cauliflower, Brussels sprouts and broccoli) is thought to be the first vegetable to be cultivated and has been used as both food and medicine for thousands of years. The Greeks considered cabbage to be a wonderful tonic and rejuvenator – they even used it as a cure for baldness! Cabbage juice is a naturopathic favourite and often used as a cleansing tonic. It contains good amounts of carotenoids (notably beta-carotene) and vitamins C, E and K, and is rich in calcium, magnesium and potassium, sulphur, phosphorus, chlorine and iodine. The combination of sulphur and chlorine has a cleansing action on the stomach and intestines. Calcium helps build healthy bones and teeth and can also help protect against osteoporosis.

Cabbage juice is an effective laxative and cleansing skin food, as well as being used for its soothing and healing effects on stomach ulcers and hiatal hernias. Back in the 1950s Dr Garnett Cheney, of the Stanford University Medical School in California, found raw cabbage juice to be an effective cure for peptic stomach ulcers. However, some might find cabbage juice causes flatulence (wind) because it contains a high amount of sulphur, which reacts with the intestinal bacteria and can produce mild gas. If this happens, try diluting the juice with water or apple or carrot juice.

Buying and preparing:
Cabbages are available throughout the year and keep well in a cool place or the fridge. Look for fresh, firm cabbages without damaged or wilted outside leaves. The darker the cabbage, the greater the nutritional value. All cabbages should be washed before juicing.

Juice rating:
170ml per 450g of cabbage

Brassica oleracea KALE

Kale was one of the first members of the brassica family to be cultivated as an edible crop and it shares many of the same nutrients and therapeutic properties as other family members, including cabbage, broccoli, cauliflower, Brussels sprouts, mustard, etc. Kale is particularly notable for its high calcium content – gram for gram kale juice has as much usable calcium as milk, which makes it a valuable source for vegans and those with allergies to dairy products. Like other brassicas, kale is rich in vitamins and minerals, including sulphur, which helps benefit the skin and hair.

Buying and preparing
Choose bright-green, fresh, crisp leaves. They need to be washed before juicing. Kale is available most of the year and stores well in the fridge.

Juice rating:
170ml per 450g of kale

Brassica rapa TURNIP

Turnips are another type of brassica. They are eaten mostly for their tender bulbous root, although the leafy tops are highly nutritious and very tasty as well. Native to Russia, Siberia and Scandinavia, the most popular variety is the purple-top white globe. In northern England and Scotland, turnips are known as neeps, a term also used to describe the larger, yellow variety recognised more widely as swede. Turnips are rich in beta-carotene, lutein and zeaxanthin and are a good source of vitamin C, B vitamins, calcium and magnesium.

The juice is considered especially good for mucus or catarrhal conditions and is useful in helping to treat asthma and other bronchial disturbances. However, the leafy green tops stand out among all other vegetables for their calcium content, which makes them an excellent source of this valuable mineral for young children or those with brittle or weak bones. Gram for gram, turnip-top juice contains more calcium than milk. For best absorption in the body, calcium needs to have magnesium present and so it is a good idea to mix the green leaves with a magnesium-rich vegetable such as dandelion, cabbage or green peppers. For those suffering from haemorrhoids, a mixture of turnip, carrot, watercress and spinach juice is said to provide soothing relief.

Buying and preparing:
Don't let the turnip tops get away because they contain 90 per cent of the nutrients! The root should be firm and the leaves dark green.

Juice extraction:
114–170ml per 450g of turnip root or per bunch of leaves

Capsicum, sweet or bell peppers belong to the *Solanaceae* or nightshade family that also includes tobacco, potatoes, tomatoes and aubergines, introduced to Europe from South and Central America. Despite being a member of a potentially poisonous group of plants, peppers are a wonderfully protective food and contain many nutrients that help build up our immune system – notably beta-carotene and vitamin C. The amount of vitamin C they contain compares with that found in oranges and grapefruits, therefore pepper in your diet helps to promote good health and ward off colds.

Green peppers will usually turn into red peppers if left to ripen, and some naturopaths advise we should only eat red peppers as the green ones are unripe and not ready to be eaten. (There is one variety however, called Permagreen, which, as its name suggests, simply stays green.) Red peppers have twice the vitamin C content of green peppers and slightly higher levels of other compounds, including the skin-protecting antioxidant lycopene. All bell peppers contain high levels of the 'beauty element' silicon, which gives us healthy hair, skin, nails and teeth. Apparently fruit and vegetables with shiny skins are rich in silicon and potassium, which is

certainly true in the case of peppers. This combination of nutrients not only enhances our looks, but also stimulates the blood circulation to help tone and cleanse the arteries and heart.

Note: some may find themselves mildly affected by vegetables in the nightshade family, especially those with arthritis and joint problems who may find their condition aggravated by these foods, since they can react adversely to the solanine content.

Buying and preparing:
The best peppers to use for juicing are the sweet or bell peppers, which come in an array of bright colours – green, red, yellow, orange and black. The differences in colour come from different seed stocks and cultivars. Choose peppers that are smooth, firm and crisp with shiny skins, but if they are too suspiciously shiny they may have been waxed and are therefore best avoided. Peppers are available all year round, they store well in the fridge and only need a quick wash before juicing. Pepper juice is pretty strong to taste and is best diluted with other juices, such as tomato or carrot.

Juice extraction:
114–170ml per 450g of peppers

Carica papaya PAPAYA

Papayas are native to Mexico and Central America and have smooth, buttery flesh that is especially rich in beta-carotene, folic acid, lycopene, polyphenols, vitamins C and K, and the minerals calcium, phosphorus, magnesium and potassium.

What distinguishes papaya from most other fruit is its incredible digestive properties. Papayas are rich in papain, a protein-digesting enzyme, which is so effective that it is used in meat tenderisers and digestants. The juice has a marvellous effect on stomach ulcers and fevers and many people consider papayas to be the great rejuvenator, combating premature ageing. This ability to rejuvenate may be due to the fact that poor digestion leads to malnourished cells, whereas efficient digestion ensures that the cells are properly fed.

Taken as a digestive aid, papaya juice has been known to correct stomach upsets extremely quickly. As early as the 1930s doctors were using papain to treat allergies. By improving the body's ability to digest food properly, papain increases allergic tolerance. Papaya mixes well with pineapple, which also contains digestive enzymes. If you are using papaya primarily for its digestive properties, buy it when it is still green as an unripe papaya contains more active papain than a ripe one.

Another reason to juice papaya is its ability to help restore a healthy balance of bacteria in the gut after a course of antibiotics. Papaya juice may also be a good blood tonic, by helping to prevent blood clots forming, and it makes an effective laxative and cleanser of the liver, kidneys and intestines, due to its ability to dissolve excess mucus in the body.

Buying and preparing:
In some outlets papayas may be labelled as pawpaws. Shaped like pears with a green or yellow skin, ripe papayas yield a little when squeezed. Before juicing, cut them in half and scoop out the orange-yellow flesh, discarding the seeds and skin.

Juice rating:
28–85ml per 450g of papaya

Cichorium endivia ENDIVE (CHICORY)

The endive, also known as frisée lettuce, is native to South and South East Asia. It is a green, curly-leaved, lettuce-like vegetable and is generally eaten raw in salads. Naturally slightly bitter, endive is rich in folic acid, beta-carotene, vitamin K and potassium, and makes a useful appetite stimulant because of its bitter ingredients. It is also reputed to be an effective cleanser of the liver, kidneys and bladder and has been used to treat hay fever and asthma and to clear up skin problems. Endives are similar to dandelions in nutrient value and as both vegetables tend to bitterness they are best mixed with other sweeter vegetable juices such as carrot, celery and parsley.

Because of its name, there is often confusion between proper endive (frisée lettuce) and the small, smooth leaves of the Belgian endive. The latter has whitish leaves with green or purple-tips, and is actually the cultivated variety of common chicory. This too can be juiced, although it contains fewer nutrients.

Buying and preparing:
Buy fresh-looking green leaves. Endive needs washing before juicing. It stores well in the fridge.

Juice rating:
114–170ml per 450g of endive

Citrullus lanatus WATERMELON – SEE MELON *(Cucumis melo)*

Citrus aurantifolia, Citrus limon LIME & LEMON

Lemons and limes are probably best known for their high vitamin C content, which was responsible for curing British sailors of scurvy. Long before vitamin C had been identified Captain Cook ensured that citrus fruits were issued to his crew – hence the nickname 'Limey' which refers to sailors who ate limes on long voyages. Attesting to the wonders of citrus fruits, nearly all of Captain Cook's crews returned to their home port alive in an age when just half of the crew was expected to survive a voyage.

Lemons and limes are two of the most highly alkalising of the citrus fruits and have an exceptionally high vitamin C content. They contain up to four times the amount of citric acid as oranges or grapefruit. This high citric acid content is wonderful for helping rid the system of waste matter. Lemons are good for soothing sore throats and catarrhal conditions and have traditionally been used as a cure for colds and 'flu. Both fruits tend to direct eliminations through the skin, which naturopaths use to help heal fevers. As with grapefruit, lemons and limes are also rich in pectin and bioflavonoids.

Buying and preparing:
The brighter and shinier the fruit, the more likely it is to be waxed. Try to buy unwaxed fruits with thin skins that feel heavy for their size. Unless organic, lemons and limes should be peeled before juicing, taking care to leave on the pith. They store well in the fridge.

Juice rating:
114–142ml per 450g of lemons or limes

Citrus paradisi GRAPEFRUIT

Grapefruits belong to the citrus family, which includes lemons, oranges, limes, tangerines, clementines and satsumas. Like all citrus fruits, they have a high vitamin C content. This makes them a valuable weapon in warding off colds and infections, and helping to prevent bleeding gums. Grapefruit is also a good source of beta-carotene, phosphorus, calcium and potassium. High levels of pectin, which is renowned for controlling cholesterol levels and helping with digestive problems, are found in the white pith. Bioflavonoids are found in the pith and work to boost the effect of vitamin C. They also have anti-inflammatory properties and they help protect the blood vessels and capillaries. Opt for the pink or ruby red grapefruit – they're also a good source of lycopene.

When using any of the citrus fruits for juicing, remember they are highly eliminative and should be used sparingly, otherwise they could stir up too many eliminations at once and leave you with skin eruptions, diarrhoea and an irritated nervous system! Citrus juices taken in excess can leach calcium from the bones and teeth, especially in those with a lowered metabolism, such as people who are ill, the elderly and those with a sedentary lifestyle. The cleansing action and nutrient value of grapefruits are similar to oranges, making them a good alternative if oranges are causing allergic reactions.

Note: eating the fruit or drinking grapefruit juice can affect some medications, so if you have been prescribed medicine, check with your GP or pharmacist to see if your prescription is among those that can be affected by grapefruit and grapefruit juice.

Buying and preparing:
Buy ripe, juicy grapefruits that have thin skins and feel heavy for their size. The pink varieties contain up to 16 times more beta-carotene and lycopene than the more common yellow ones. Peel before juicing, but be careful not to remove too much of the nutrient-rich pith. If peeling with a knife, just remove the shiny outer skin and keep the white pith beneath. Grapefruits store well in the fridge or a cool, dark pantry and can be bought in bulk to reduce the cost.

Juice rating:
170–227ml per 450g of grapefruit

Oranges, along with grapes, are one of the oldest fruits known in history and are one of the most popular juices. However, all too often commercially prepared juices give you just the orange 'flavour' and little of the vitality or nutrients of the fruit. Oranges are one of the richest sources of vitamin C (although don't forget the humble kiwi fruit, which has double the amount) and it is their ability to help protect against a variety of conditions from winter colds to heart disease that gives them such a high health rating. Studies carried out by the National Cancer Institute in America showed that those who ate the most oranges, compared to those who ate the fewest, had the lowest incidence of developing cancer. As an antioxidant, vitamin C helps mop up damaging free radicals which age the skin and cause premature wrinkles and sagging.

As with grapefruit, you need to peel before juicing, being careful to leave as much of the pith on as possible, since this is where many of the nutrients are, including vitamin C, beta-carotene and the B-complex vitamins, bioflavonoids, pectin, amino acids, potassium, zinc and phosphorus.

Vitamin C helps the body absorb iron better, so a glass of orange juice a day can actually double the amount of iron available for use in the body (especially if eaten with a boiled egg, for example – the perfect breakfast combination!). The high citric acid content in oranges is most effective in cleansing the gastrointestinal tract and aiding the elimination of toxins and acid wastes from cells. For this reason, freshly squeezed orange juice is frequently included in eliminative diets.

Together vitamin C and bioflavonoids act as anti-coagulants, strengthen the blood vessels and capillaries, and help ward off colds and 'flu. Both the heart and lungs benefit from regular drinking of orange juice. What better way to increase your supply of vitamin C in the winter months than by drinking a glass of fresh juice?

Buying and preparing:
Look for firm, heavy oranges with bright, fresh-looking skin. Avoid those with damaged or wrinkled dry skin. Oranges are available throughout the year and keep well in a cool place.

Juice rating:
170–227ml per 450g of oranges

Melons belong to the same family as cucumbers and squash and, like cucumbers, have a cooling effect on the body. Their root systems reach deep into the soil, which makes them one of the most mineral-rich fruits around.

Melons are an excellent fruit for juicing because of their high water content. This also makes them a first-class diuretic, wonderful kidney cleanser and skin purifier. As with many other fruit and vegetables, most of the nutrients lie in the flesh right next to the skin, so be careful not to lose this part when peeling. Melon juice has a light, sweet taste and mixes well with other juices. You could use it to sweeten sour juices or to dilute thick ones.

Of the many varieties of melon to choose, including cantaloupe, honeydew, galia and watermelon, the orange-fleshed cantaloupes are the most nutritious. High in beta-carotene, vitamin C and digestive enzymes, they are highly recommended by the American Cancer Society as a healthful agent against intestinal cancer. Watermelons, as you might expect, have the highest water content and are fabulous natural diuretics as well as being packed with skin-enriching minerals such as zinc and potassium.

Buying and preparing:
Choose ripe, firm melons. As a general test, the blossom end should give slightly when ripe and they should have a pleasant aroma. It is hard to tell a ripe watermelon without cutting it open, however; the flesh should be firm and juicy and with a good red colour. Before juicing, cut off the flesh as close to the skin as possible and remove the seeds.

Juice rating:
170–227ml per 450g of melon

Cucumis sativus CUCUMBER

Cucumbers, originally yellow in colour, came from India where they were celebrated as a symbol of fertility. Other members of the same family include pumpkins and marrows. The old saying 'as cool as a cucumber' aptly describes their blood-cooling powers – on a warm day, the interior of a cucumber can be as much as 20°C cooler than the outside air temperature. They make a wonderful digestive aid and have a cleansing effect on the bowels and skin. The high water content makes cucumber a powerful diuretic and kidney cleanser. Cucumber and carrot juice is often used to ease the symptoms of rheumatism as it helps to eliminate excess uric acid in the joints.

Cucumbers are rich in potassium, which helps give skin cells their elasticity to keep us looking younger. The high potassium content also makes them a valuable aid in regulating either high or low blood pressure. Cucumber juice is a good source of silicon and sulphur, the minerals that promote healthy hair, skin and nails. Most of the vitamin A (in the form of beta-carotene) is found in the skin of the cucumber so, as long as they are organic and neither waxed nor sprayed, it's far better to juice them unpeeled. If you do have to remove the skin, you can make up for the lost beta-carotene by mixing in some carrot juice.

Buying and preparing:
Look for unwaxed cucumbers that feel firm to the touch. They need to be washed before juicing and will store well in the fridge. Cucumbers are grown in greenhouses and are therefore available throughout the year. Curved cucumbers are often less expensive than their ruler-straight counterparts and just as good for juicing.

Juice rating:
114–170ml per 450g of cucumber

Daucus carota CARROT

There are over 3,000 species in the carrot family, including celery, fennel and parsnip and the herbs parsley, dill and coriander. Carrots have been cultivated for thousands of years and will grow almost anywhere in their native Europe. They are just as happy in the sandy soil of windswept coastlines as in the relative calm of the back garden plot. The firmness of the growing soil largely determines their shape though – light, sandy soil allows for long, slender roots to burrow through the earth as they grow, whereas heavy clay soils grow stubbier, fatter carrots. Whatever the shape, the British love carrots and eat more per person than any other country in the world. Many of us will remember being told to eat our carrots because they help us see in the dark, on account of their high beta-carotene content. In fact, carrots were dished up during the Second World War in aerial-training schools allegedly to improve the eyesight of the students. In actual fact, the rumour was propagated to throw the enemy off the scent because the Royal Air Force had the newly invented advantage of Radar!

Carrots are a mainstay kitchen ingredient of any committed juicer. Breaking down the vegetable cell walls contained within carrots releases more available nutrients than chomping raw carrot sticks. Cooked carrots are actually more nutritious than raw carrots, as the nutrients contained within the vegetable cell walls are broken down by heating in a similar way. Because carrots are a source of the three main antioxidant vitamins, A (in the form of beta-carotene), C and E, their juice often forms the basis of anti-cancer diets. American cancer specialist Dr JL Freudenheim asserts 'eating a carrot a day can raise beta-carotene levels enough to give considerable protection'. Carrot juice has many other therapeutic features, including the ability to soothe and tone the intestinal walls, strengthen bones and teeth, stimulate digestion, cleanse the blood and act as a diuretic. It also keeps our eyes bright and our skin clear. Perhaps its most important gift to our wellbeing and beauty is its restorative and cleansing effect on the liver. Part of the liver's job is to deal with fats and oils, and drinking carrot juice helps to reduce the damaging fat and cholesterol levels in the blood. In addition to their high antioxidant content, carrots also contain many of the B vitamins, as well as essential minerals such as calcium, iron, potassium, sodium and phosphorus.

Carrot juice gives sweetness to some of the more bitter vegetable juices and, like apple juice, makes a perfect base for almost any juice combination.

Buying and preparing:
Carrots are available all year round and should be firm and crisp, not tired-looking. If they come with their feathery tops attached, remove these quickly as they take nutrients from the roots (you can add the tops to your juice as well). Carrots keep well in a cool place or in the fridge.

Juice rating:
170–227ml per 450g of carrots

Foeniculum vulgare FENNEL

Fennel is an odd-looking vegetable with a distinctive and somewhat surprising aniseed flavour. It was popular in the Middle Ages, more for warding off evil spirits and witches than as a food. Today it is a well-loved salad vegetable in Mediterranean countries – the French also use it to treat headaches and dizziness. There are two types: garden fennel, which grows tall and is mainly used as a herb; and Florence fennel, a white bulb with a bright-green feathery top. It's the Florence fennel that makes a lovely aromatic juice.

As a member of the same family as celery, fennel shares many of the same nutrients and properties. It contains an impressive amount of beta-carotene, folic acid and vitamin C as well as traces of iron, calcium and magnesium. The calcium and magnesium content is what gives fennel juice its wonderfully calming and relaxing properties.

Naturopaths often cite fennel as being a good blood builder with great therapeutic effect in cases of menstrual disorders, particularly when it is mixed with carrot and beetroot juice. Like celery, fennel also contains essential oils that can be helpful in treating stomach upsets and flatulence.

Buying and preparing:
A fresh fennel bulb should be firm and white with bright-green feathery leaves on top. Before juicing, wash well. All parts can be juiced. Fennel is available throughout the year and can be stored in the fridge. It adds a pleasant flavour to other vegetable juices.

Juice rating:
170–227ml per 450g of Florence fennel

Fragaria ananassa STRAWBERRY

Strawberries, native to the Americas, are now cultivated worldwide and what a deliciously sweet and juicy way to pack in a wonderful source of vitamins and minerals! Their high levels of beta-carotene, manganese and vitamin C help fight off colds and infections, and can also help prevent cancer and heart disease, while potassium and iron help to strengthen the blood. They are cleansing and eliminative, which makes them a great spring cleaner. They have also been found to relieve arthritis – by fasting on strawberries the renowned Swedish botanist Linnaeus is said to have cured himself of this painful condition. Some are allergic to cultivated strawberries, but may be able to tolerate the smaller 'wild' strawberry. Strawberry juice is fairly thick and sweet and is best diluted with other juices or used to flavour less strong-tasting juices.

Buying and preparing:
Locally grown strawberries are widely available in the UK summer months and are preferable to imported fruits, as they are likely to be fresher and therefore richer in vitamin C and other nutrients. Some imported strawberries may also have been irradiated to prolong shelf life after transit and this also depletes vitamin content (irradiation should be clearly printed on a label). Buy the berries when they are plump, firm and bright red with the green top still on. They need to be washed before juicing and can be stored for a few days in the fridge; however, the vitamin C content will diminish the longer they are stored.

Juice rating:
114–142ml per 450g of strawberries

Lactuca sativa LETTUCE

Lettuce is one of the oldest vegetables and is thought to have originated in India or Central Asia. Both its name in English and in Latin (*Lactuca*) refer to its milky white juice or latex. Incidentally, this contains mild sedative properties long known to herbalists (which is why Peter Rabbit fell asleep in Mr McGregor's garden having eaten his lettuces). Lettuce is both juicy and flavoursome. The dark-leaved varieties, including cos, radicchio, lamb's leaf, oak leaf, and other grow-your-own traditional types are the most nutritious. Despite its popularity, the commercially produced iceberg is one of the least nutritious varieties. When selecting lettuces for juicing, bear in mind that dark-leaved varieties can contain up to 50 times the nutrients of light-green or white-leaved lettuces, so colour counts.

Dark green lettuce leaves are a good source of calcium, magnesium, iron, potassium, silicon, beta-carotene, vitamin E and chlorophyll. In particular, a high silicon content means lettuce can help to add shine and thickness to hair and a glow to the skin. Some claim that a glass of lettuce juice a day even helps restores hair loss! True or not, all the minerals lettuce juice contains certainly benefit our looks and wellbeing.

The magnesium in lettuce is exceptionally energising, particularly for our muscles, brain and nerves, and the phosphorus and sulphur content also helps to calm nervous dispositions. Like most green vegetable juices, lettuce is quite bitter on its own and tastes better if it is mixed with other juices – carrot and spinach, for example.

Buying and preparing: Lettuce should be washed well, but not left to soak as this depletes its nutrient content. Washing it is really important as, according to the US National Research Council, lettuce is one of the main sources of pesticide residues in our diet. Always wash pre-packed, bagged salads and chopped lettuce leaves as they are more likely to be tainted with traces of chlorine used in processing to prolong shelf-life.

To make it easier to juice leafy vegetables such as lettuce, roll the leaves into balls and then push them into the juicer along with a piece of carrot or a chunk of apple to help force them through.

Juice rating:
57–227ml per 450g of lettuce. Heavier varieties make more juice than the looser-leaved types.

Malus domestica APPLE

One of the first things we English speakers learn is 'A' is for apple and it's also one of the first fruits we eat. Countless generations of babies have been weaned on a spoonful of apple purée. Apples have been around for thousands of years and feature in many legends and religious stories. Hieroglyphic writings found in the pyramids and tombs of ancient Egypt show that apples were used both as a food and as a medicine. Today, with over 1,000 types to choose from, including both summer and winter varieties, apples are available all year round. China is a major apple grower, producing around half the world's apple supplies, followed by the United States. The harder, crisper kinds are better for juicing but all are a terrific source of pectin, tannic acid and malic acid, which help to remove toxins from the intestines and regulate the bowel. Their potassium and phosphorus content helps keep the liver and kidneys working healthily and the skin looking fresh and clear.

There has to be some truth in the maxim 'an apple a day keeps the doctor away' because apples are a good source of beta-carotene, lutein and zeaxanthin, which together with vitamins C and K, and the mineral magnesium help to ward off colds and infections. Apples are considered powerful blood purifiers and benefit both the blood and lymphatic systems. Apple juice is a wonderful cleanser, great for weight-reducing diets and useful as an all-round general tonic.

Buying and preparing:
Apples should be firm and crisp; avoid bruised or damaged ones. They should be stored in a cool, dry place and need to be washed before juicing. Apple juice mixes well with most other juices and can help thin out strong-tasting juices, such as beetroot, or thick juices such as prune and strawberry.

Juice rating:
170–227ml per 450g of apples

Mangifera indica MANGO

Scented and richly flavoured, mangoes are one of the most delicious fruits in the world and yield a wonderful bright orange-yellow juice. Those living in northern climes have to pay a relatively high price for mangoes, but in tropical regions where they flourish, such as Africa, Asia and the Caribbean they are cheap and plentiful.

Mangoes are rich in beta-carotene, lutein, zeaxanthin, vitamin C and potassium. The riper the fruit, the more beta-carotene the mango will contain – which accounts for the glorious orange-coloured flesh. The mango is said to be a great blood cleanser and it is hoped that recent studies into the properties of mango skin may lead to advances in some cancer treatments.

Buying and preparing:
Buy ripe mangoes, which give a little when pressed (like an avocado). Avoid bruised or damaged fruit. Another test for ripeness is their unmistakably sweet fragrance, so take a sniff before you buy if you want to eat it that day. Mangoes vary in colour from green and yellow to orange and red. Peel and remove the stone before juicing. Mangoes are tropical fruits and are best stored at room temperature. Their juice is sweet and thick and can be thinned out with other juices such as apple or orange.

Juice rating:
57ml per medium-sized mango

Nasturtium officinale WATERCRESS

This is yet another member of the brassica family, which includes cabbage, turnips, broccoli, etc. Closely related to garden cress, mustard and radish, watercress thrives in watery conditions and lime-rich soil. A native of South America, it has long been used in Brazil for its therapeutic effects on tuberculosis and when it came to Europe the Romans used it as a hair tonic.

Watercress is one of the super foods that, leaf for leaf, gives so much. It is rich in iron, calcium, iodine and folic acid, as well as beta-carotene, vitamins C and E. It is also high in the nutrients that help with catarrhal conditions and is being researched for its potential anti-cancer properties. It is a good blood purifier and encourages glandular secretions. Watercress is a great health restorer and has a really positive effect on the digestive system, gall bladder and liver. It is a powerful cleanser with an equally potent taste, so needs to be diluted with other vegetable juices such as celery and carrot.

Watercress contains some of the highest amounts of sulphur compared with other vegetables, which makes it a must-have for healthy skin and hair. Watercress also contains large amounts of chlorophyll, which helps to oxygenate the blood and cleanse the system. It may also be useful in weight-loss programmes, too, as the juice is thought to stimulate the metabolism.

Buying and preparing:
Watercress leaves should be bright green and fresh looking. They need to be washed before use and can be stored in the fridge. Keep damp and sealed in an airtight bag or container. Watercress is commercially farmed in purpose built ponds and is available most of the year.

Juice rating:
28–57ml per average-sized bunch of watercress

Pastinaca sativa PARSNIP

Parsnips look a little like pale-coloured carrots and were once the staple food of Europe's poor. They have a carbohydrate content similar to potatoes, but a nutritional value more akin to carrots (minus the beta-carotene). Parsnips are great bowel regulators and have a beneficial effect on the liver, which makes them a useful addition in detox diets. They are also reputed to be mildly diuretic and anti-arthritic. The great herbalist Culpeper (1653) states: 'The garden parsnip nourished much and is good and wholesome, but a little windy. It is good for stomach and reins [kidney] and provoketh urine'.

The juice is rich in vitamin C, potassium, manganese, phosphorus, sulphur and silicon, and these last two nutrients make it a wonderful tonic for the skin, hair and nails – its silicon content being especially good for brittle nails. Like carrot, parsnip juice is sweet, but it also has a distinctive nutty taste. It is a good juice for adding sweetness and flavour to bitter and less tasty vegetable juices.

Buying and preparing:
Choose firm roots and store in a cool place. Parsnips need to be scrubbed before juicing. Do not peel as most of the nutrients lie just beneath the skin.

Juice rating:
114–170ml per 450g of parsnips

Prunus armeniaca APRICOT

Apricots are one of the staple foods of the remote Hunza people of the Himalayas, famous for their fitness, health and longevity. That would seem reason enough to make them a regular feature in your diet! Fresh apricots are only available for a short window during the summer months – but the odd dried apricot can be added to a juicing mixture for taste and a shot of readily absorbed vegetal iron. The healthiest option are the dark-brown dried apricots as these are not treated with sulphur dioxide, a preservative that can cause skin allergies.

Apricots are one of the beta-carotene champions of the fruit world and therefore stand out among other fruits as cancer fighters. They may help prevent cancer of the lung, oesophagus, stomach, bladder and throat, and their high vitamin C content also helps protect against colds and 'flu.

Buying and preparing:
Apricots have a short season and are best picked when completely ripe to ensure maximum beta-carotene and B vitamin content. They should be a uniform golden-orange colour and yield to slight pressure. Fresh, ripe apricots should be plump and juicy, not wizened, soft or mushy. Wash and stone the fruit before juicing. Apricots do not keep for long and need to be stored in a cool place.

Juice extacted:
57ml per 450g of apricots

Prunus domestica PRUNE

Prunes are dried or semi-dried plums and their high concentration of phenolic compounds means they are widely used as a natural laxative. Prune juice is just as potent as the whole fruit and is a more natural and healthier way to treat constipation than using synthetic laxatives. Prunes are also a good source of the antioxidants vitamins C and E, as well as vitamin K, folic acid and calcium.

Buying and preparing:
It is best to buy prunes which are not oiled or preserved with sulphur dioxide, and which are already pitted. To get the most out of dried prunes, soak them overnight in warm water and juice them the following day together with the prune-rich water. Semi-dried prunes can be juiced without overnight soaking, although soaking will provide more liquid matter for juicing. Prune juice is quite thick, however it can be diluted with other juices such as apple, for example.

Juice rating:
Varies – depending on how much water is used for soaking

Prunus persica PEACH

Peaches have been cultivated for over 4,000 years and are thought to have originally come from China. If conditions are right, a peach tree can live for hundreds of years. Like other yellow-coloured fruits, peaches are an excellent source of beta-carotene. They also contain vitamin C, some of the B vitamins (including folic acid) and minerals such as calcium, phosphorus and potassium.

Peach juice is wonderfully alkalising and useful for cleansing the intestinal tract as well as encouraging good bowel movement. It tastes extremely sweet and a little goes a long way flavour-wise.

Buying and preparing:
Choose ripe, un-bruised peaches and avoid fruit that is overripe, green or damaged. To prepare: wash well, cut in half and remove the stone. Peach juice is fairly thick and may need to be thinned out with other juices such as apple and orange.

Juice rating:
28–85ml per 450g of peaches. The riper the peach, the more juice it will yield; if you have an option, go for the riper, squashier fruits.

Pyrus communis PEAR

Pears are native to Europe and one variety or another is available most of the year round. Their sweetness makes them ideal for mixing with more bitter or tart juices. Pears have one of the least allergenic profiles of any fruit, making them a favourite for exclusion diets when screening for dietary allergies. They are also low in salicylates and benzoates. Like many tree fruit, pears are a good source of vitamin C and the B vitamins as well as potassium, phosphorus and calcium. The juice is a wonderful digestive aid and, when juiced with the skin on, provides good amounts of dietary fibre, which helps to normalise the bowel. Pear is a valuable addition to elimination diets because of its mild diuretic and laxative effect. Pear juice is considered to be one of the best urinary and gastrointestinal cleansers because of its high level of pectin.

Buying and preparing:
Buy pears that are still firm to the touch and avoid overripe or bruised ones. Overripe pears may clog up your juicer and do not provide as much juice. Pears can be kept in the fridge for up to a week. Before juicing, wash the outside well and cut into quarters.

Juice rating:
114–170ml per 450g of pears

Raphanus sativus RADISH

Radishes are part of the same family as cabbages and cauliflowers, and feature in ancient Egyptian records as a most popular food. Images carved on the temples at Karnak include radishes, while a solid-gold statue of a radish once stood in the temple at Delphi.

Radish juice is strongly diuretic and stimulates the appetite and digestion. It helps get rid of excess mucus in the sinuses and gastrointestinal tract by its cleansing and soothing action on the mucus membranes. A mixture of radish and carrot juice is especially beneficial in this respect. Radishes are rich in vitamin C, potassium, calcium and magnesium. They help break down gallstones and cleanse the kidneys, liver and gall bladder. A juice cocktail of radish, cucumber and green pepper is especially good for the latter. They are easy to grow on a kitchen windowsill and start to sprout from seed to plant in as little as three days, which makes them a good crop for a children's garden, alongside carrots.

Buying and preparing:
Radishes should be fresh-looking, crisp and red. If they come with their green leaves, cut these off as soon as possible, as they draw the nutrients from the roots; add them to your juicing mixture if you wish. Radishes are available throughout the year and can be stored in the fridge. The juice is very strong and is best mixed with other juices such as carrot or cucumber.

Juice rating:
57–114ml per 450g of radishes

Rubus fruticosus BLACKBERRY

Blackberries are a rich source of vitamin C, with good amounts of beta-carotene, B vitamins, vitamin K and the minerals potassium, calcium and manganese, which makes them invaluable in helping to prevent heart disease, cancer, high blood pressure and premenstrual tension. Blackberries also have a high vegetal iron content, which makes them one of the finest blood builders.

Buying and preparing:
Look for plump, dark blackberries – red ones are not ripe and will not give much juice. Beware of picking roadside blackberries since fruit absorbs poisonous car exhaust fumes. Berries do not keep for long and are prone to mould so it is best to use them as soon as possible and pick early in the season when you can. Fresh, ripe blackberries add a wonderfully rich colour and flavour to other juices. They also freeze well for using later in the year.

Juice rating:
85–114ml per 450g of blackberries

Rubus idaeus RASPBERRY

Raspberries are good internal cleansers – especially for mucus and catarrhal conditions. Their natural astringency can help sort out upset stomachs, bowel problems and gum disease. Raspberries are high in vitamin C and beta-carotene, and contain useful amounts of potassium, calcium and magnesium, which makes them invaluable in cases of heart problems, fatigue or depression. The vibrantly coloured juice has a wonderful flavour and a raspberry-juice cocktail before meals stimulates the appetite and aids digestion. Despite their sweet taste, raspberries, like other berries, are fairly low in carbohydrates and consequently they have a low glycaemic index. Eating foods that are identified as having a low glycaemic index value helps avoid swings in blood sugar levels.

Buying and preparing:
Choose fresh, plump berries that are not damaged or mushy. Raspberries are only around for a relatively short time and do not keep fresh for long, although they store well in the freezer for juicing during the winter months.

Juice rating:
114ml per 450g of raspberries

Solanum lycopersicum TOMATO

Like the potato, tomatoes are native to the Andes region of South America and were brought to Europe from Peru after the Spanish Conquest. They, too, belong to the *Solanaceae* or nightshade family and were initially thought to be poisonous.

Botanically, tomatoes are fruits and have an acid content similar to oranges and grapefruits, which means they have an alkalising effect on the body when eaten raw. They are considered to be a good blood and liver cleanser and form a valuable part of any detox diet. Those with arthritis or gout may want to avoid tomato juice altogether or dilute it with other vegetable juices in case it triggers high uric acid levels. Tomatoes contain excellent amounts of vitamins, and are particularly high in vitamin C, beta-carotene and the skin-saving compounds lycopene, lutein and zeaxanthin (the latter two are noted for their beneficial effect on eye health). Note: for some people, tomatoes can be the cause of food intolerance and can trigger skin rashes.

Buying and preparing:
Tomatoes are available throughout the year and store well in the fridge. Always select bright red, firm, naturally ripened fruit. Locally grown varieties are more likely to be naturally ripened, as are stalks of vine-ripened tomatoes. Never use unripe green tomatoes (or tomato leaves or stems) as these contain the toxic alkaloid tomatine, which can damage the kidneys.

Organic tomatoes are definitely preferable since intensively grown ones may contain high levels of pesticide residue. The US National Research Council has discovered that the pesticides commonly found in tomatoes have the greatest potential for causing cancer.

Juice extraction:
227–284ml per 450g of tomatoes

Solanum tuberosum POTATO

Potatoes originally came from the Andean regions of tropical America – an area stretching from Chile to Mexico. They belong to the *Solanaceae* or nightshade family and, like their relatives, peppers, tomatoes and aubergines, they were first brought to Europe after the Spanish Conquest. Sir Walter Raleigh brought the first potato to England and they are now one of the world's most valuable vegetable crops, with over 5,000 different varieties grown worldwide. Dr Bernard Jensen, one of America's leading nutritionists, says: 'I believe that if we had to confine ourselves to one food, the potato is the one on which we could live almost indefinitely.'

The humble potato is packed with minerals and vitamins, especially when eaten raw. Potato juice is a great internal cleanser and has a soothing effect on stomach ulcers and other digestive problems. It has proved successful in clearing up some skin blemishes, even cases of eczema. The rich potassium content is good for the liver and kidneys, and helps keep the skin elastic and the muscles supple. Potassium is the body's 'healer' and is needed for rejuvenation. A combination of potato and carrot juice makes a good internal cleanser.

Potatoes are also rich in vitamin C (they rank just below citrus fruits as an important source of vitamin C), as well as B vitamins, calcium, magnesium, phosphorus and sulphur, with traces of iron and zinc. Organic potatoes, grown in nutrient-dense soils, contain more nutrients than chemically or intensively farmed potatoes.

Many naturopaths recommend eating potatoes raw since many of the nutrients are lost or destroyed by cooking. Raw potatoes also contain easily digestible natural sugars, whereas during cooking these sugars are converted into starch. For these reasons, raw potato is an interesting addition to juicing recipes.

Buying and preparing:
Choose firm potatoes without any signs of damage and look for ones that have 'eyes', since these will be capable of sprouting and so will be filled with enzymes and vitality. It is important to avoid already sprouted or green potatoes, though, because they will have accumulated a toxic substance called solanine, which can cause headaches and nausea. Organic potatoes are definitely preferable because non-organically grown ones tend to contain traces of chemical residues, including post-harvest fungicide and anti-sprouting herbicide sprays, that washing cannot remove. New potatoes, including Jersey Royals, have come in for criticism for excessive use of toxic pesticides (which is perhaps why they appear so perfect). Again, choose new potatoes that are certified organic. The bulk of a potato's nutrients lie just below the skin, so it is best not to peel them – just scrub well before juicing. All potatoes need to be kept in a cool, dry, dark place and removed from any plastic packaging so they don't 'sweat'. Store in the dark in a wicker potato hopper, a basket or paper bags.

Juice extraction:
114–170ml per 450g of potatoes

Spinacia oleracea SPINACH

Spinach was introduced to Europe by Arab traders in the 1500s and became a favourite of Catherine de' Medici, who so favoured spinach she demanded it be served for every meal – this is why spinach dishes today are still called Florentine, reflecting Catherine's birthplace in Florence. The wonderfully rich nutritional content of spinach was made famous by Popeye, the cartoon sailor who demonstrated Herculean feats after eating a tin of spinach. However, despite being rich in iron, spinach is also high in substances including oxalate that inhibit the absorption of iron, making much of it unusable by the body. Fortunately, spinach is also an excellent source of vitamins C and E, beta-carotene, folic acid and calcium (although again, the high oxalate levels render much of the calcium useless) and it is a rich source (about 40 per cent) of potassium. Folic acid is especially important during pregnancy as it guards against spina bifida and anencephaly, a condition where the brain does not develop fully, so spinach is often recommended during the early weeks of pregnancy when a baby's neural tubes are forming. Naturopaths refer to spinach as a blood revitaliser and a great health restorer, and it is well known that drinking spinach juice is one of the best ways of dealing with constipation. Its potent cleansing and building properties strengthen and tone the liver, the gall bladder and the digestive, urinary and lymphatic systems.

Spinach is an extremely rich source of life-giving chlorophyll, which helps to fight anaemia and fatigue. Anyone with arthritis, rheumatism or gout, however, should avoid spinach juice because its high uric acid content may aggravate the condition.

Buying and preparing:
Look for crisp, bright green leaves when buying fresh. Bagged spinach is widely available all year round and can be stored for a few days in the fridge. It needs to be washed well before juicing.

Juice extraction:
114–170ml per 450g of spinach

Taraxacum officinale DANDELION

Most of us are more likely to think of dandelions as yellow-flowered weeds that clog up the lawn than as a useful juicing ingredient; however, the leaves are highly nutritious and have been used for centuries in herbal medicine. Dandelion's botanical name comes from the Greek word *taraxacum*, which means 'to stir up', and French herbalists named it *dent de lion*, or 'lion's tooth', because of its jagged leaves.

The dandelion is king of the vegetables for its beta-carotene content. It is also a rich source of vitamin C, potassium, magnesium, calcium, sodium and iron. In fact, dandelions contain as much iron as spinach and four times as much beta-carotene as lettuce. That high beta-carotene content means dandelion juice is a powerful liver cleanser and helps the flow of bile. It is also thought to be an effective diuretic. Mixing carrot and dandelion juice, for example, makes a perfect springtime tonic: magnesium is a powerful alkaliser that helps to remove acid build-up during the sedentary winter months. The magnesium content of dandelion juice also soothes and strengthens the bowel wall and the muscular and skeletal systems. The combined power of calcium and magnesium makes dandelion juice an important builder of bones and teeth. Besides this, it is used by naturopaths to help relieve the body of many toxic overload conditions that can lead to eczema and other skin inflammations.

Buying and preparing:
Dandelions are becoming more widely available commercially, but if you can't get them from the greengrocer, grow your own! Pick the young tender leaves, which are less bitter than the mature ones. Be careful to avoid roadside plants and any that are likely to have been sprayed with chemicals or wee-ed on by dogs. Dandelions taste mildest in spring and are available until early summer. The juice is believed to be one of the best spring tonics and can be sweetened with carrot or apple. Dandelion leaves will keep for a couple of days in the fridge and just need to be washed before use.

Juice extraction:
57ml per 10 dandelion leaves

Vaccinium macrocarpon CRANBERRY

Cranberries are native to the temperate and swampy regions of North America and Europe and grow wild on low thick shrubs or vines in acid soils or bogs.

Cranberry juice is commonly used for its healing properties as a natural diuretic and urinary tract cleanser, although recent research shows that it may not be helpful for some UT infections (such as cystitis) and may even worsen the condition. These sour-tasting berries do, however, contain some interesting, unusual and potentially cancer-preventing compounds, among them proanthocyanidins and quercetin (types of tannins, called polyphenols, also found in grape skins). Cranberries are a rich source of vitamin C, beta-carotene, quinine, iron and potassium. The quinine helps to maintain the health of the bladder, kidneys and prostate and may be beneficial in healing kidney conditions and helping to prevent prostate cancer. The high vitamin C and beta-carotene content helps ward off colds and 'flu in the winter months. Unlike most fruits, cranberry juice is acid-forming in the body as it converts to hippuric acid in the liver, which neutralises the usual alkalising effects of sodium, magnesium and potassium, so use sparingly. Cranberry juice also tastes pretty tart, so a good tip is to combine cranberry juice with fresh apple or carrot juice (both alkaline forming and therefore a good counter-balance for health benefits as well as taste).

Buying and preparing:
Choose firm, plump berries and avoid those that are shrivelled or damaged. They should be washed before juicing and can be stored in the fridge. Because cranberries are a winter fruit, you may wish to freeze them for use in the summer months.

Juice extraction:
114–170ml per 450g of cranberries

Vitis vinifera GRAPE

Grapes are one of the oldest fruits in history and are mentioned in the Bible as far back as the time of Noah and before. Today they are used throughout the world for their health-giving properties – and not least for making wine.

Grapes are often included in elimination and weight-loss diets because of their powerful cleansing action and their ability to stimulate the metabolism. The high magnesium content promotes good bowel movement and proper kidney function. Grape juice is also a wonderful blood and liver cleanser and is useful in eliminating unwanted uric acid from the body, making it a good choice for arthritis or rheumatism sufferers. Grapes are high in potassium, which aids kidney function, strengthens the heartbeat and keeps the skin looking fresh and healthy. They are also a useful source of beta-carotene and calcium.

Parts of France have a tradition of eating nothing but grapes during the grape harvest in order to cleanse the system and rebalance the body's acid/alkaline levels. And studies have found a lower incidence of cancer among those who practise this annual grape diet. There are fasting clinics in Germany where grapes are frequently given as a seven-day single-fruit fast with good results, especially for patients with arthritis. The so-called 'French paradox' refers to the relatively low incidence of heart disease in France despite the nation's high consumption of animal fats. It is thought that this may be partly due to types of tannins called polyphenols (such as resveratrol, proanthocyanidins and quercetin) found in grape skins.

Buying and preparing:
Grapes are one of the most over-sprayed crops around so it is far better to buy organic ones where possible, especially when the skins are being juiced. Commercially grown grapes have been known to contain residues of up to 40 different pesticides and toxic chemicals. Buy fresh, plump grapes for juicing and discard overripe, shrivelled or mouldy ones that are dropping off their stems. Grapes need to be well washed (wash in soapy water, then rinse well, especially if they are not organic) and can be stored in the fridge for up to a week. Don't worry about buying seedless varieties, since the seeds can go through the juicer as well. Grape juice mixes well with other juices and makes a good natural sweetener. On its own, grape juice is extremely sweet and so should be avoided by diabetics or those with a blood sugar disorder.

Juice extraction:
227ml per 450g of grapes

Zingiber officinale GINGER ROOT

Ginger root is a spice not a vegetable, but merits inclusion for its power to add zest and gusto to almost any juice combination. It is an essential juicing ingredient!

Since ancient times ginger has been popular in the Far East, where it is used for both its healing properties and its pungent, warming flavour. It is used extensively by practitioners of traditional Chinese herbal medicine and, in Japan, ginger root has been found to be an effective painkiller, particularly in treating chronic inflammation. Ginger wards off colds and 'flu symptoms and helps eliminate mucus from the sinuses and phlegm from the lungs. A mixture of carrot and ginger juice is great if you feel a cold coming on. Ginger's antiseptic properties help with throat problems like laryngitis and are especially useful for protecting and healing the gut, as well as treating nausea and motion sickness.

A combination of apple and ginger juice is a good antidote for travel sickness. Ginger has also been found useful in combating morning sickness.

Buying and preparing:
Ginger root should be dry and firm to the touch. It is generally available throughout the year and keeps for a week or two in a cool place. Some like to peel the pale brown skin from the knobbly root before juicing, otherwise simply scrub well. Ginger root also freezes well if you sense you are not going to use it before it goes soft.

Juice extraction:
A small cube (about 1cm) will add sufficient bite to most juice cocktails and gives a lovely flavour to melon and apple juice.

What else can you juice?

Fresh fruit and vegetables are only just the beginning for a serious juicer – here's the lowdown on some of my all-time super-food favourites.

Sprouted seeds and beans

These are easy to grow – and guaranteed organic if you do it yourself! It's also fun watching the little seeds or beans burst into life in a matter of days. The juiciest sprouts and shoots obviously juice the best, but even a handful of freshly sprouted alfalfa or cress makes a tangy addition to juice mixes. Home-grown sprouted seeds and beans provide a constant source of freshly harvested green goodness – perfect to pop into a juicer and add to recipes. Simply sprinkle seeds onto dampened kitchen towel, keep moist and wait for the little gems to sprout. Alternatively, invest in a simple germinator tray, available from good health-food shops. When seeds, peas or beans start to sprout, their stored power-house of nutrients is released in an easily absorbable form – ideal for supplying us with year-round goodness. There is a whole variety of seeds or beans you can try, such as alfalfa, cress, sesame, adzuki, mung bean, chickpea, radish, lentils and quinoa.

For those who prefer the ease and convenience of using powdered wheat grass (and other super foods), there are many new and exciting products on the market. Although they seem expensive at first glance, keep in mind that these are packs of concentrated goodness, so a little goes a very long way. I actually find these packs an easy and economical way to boost the potency and vitality of my juices.

Herbs and nettles

Herbs and other deep green plant leaves are a very valuable addition to juicing. Parsley, for example, is a rich source of vitamin C, while nettles and dandelions (mentioned previously) are wonderful internal cleansers and diuretics. Along with a piquant tang, coriander adds dietary fibre to vegetable blends and is a great detoxer, while freshly juiced basil leaves lend their antibacterial properties and a healthy dose of beta-carotene – basil is especially good with tomato and celery-based juices. These soft herbs are easy to grow and it's never difficult to find nettles and dandelions, but do make sure they are unsprayed and not growing on roadsides – gather the leaves while they are still young.

Wheat grass

Wheat grass is one of the most prized green juices of all, and a fabulous source of life-giving enzymes, chlorophyll and other essential nutrients. Many naturopaths advocate it in juices specifically prepared as part of treatment programmes for cancer sufferers and those with serious diseases. This super-juice, extracted from young blades of the wheat plant, is one of the richest sources of chlorophyll you can find; just a single shot measure of wheat grass is said to pack the same nutritional punch as a kilo of other green leafy vegetables. Wheat grass includes good levels of beta-carotene, vitamins C, E and K, the B vitamins thiamin, riboflavin, niacin, vitamin B6 and pantothenic acid, and also the minerals iron, zinc, copper, manganese and selenium.

How to grow your own wheat grass

Growing your own wheat grass can be a bit more of an undertaking than herbs and sprouted seeds or beans, but it's well worth the effort. Choose organically grown spelt wheat grass seeds (also called wheat berries or winter wheat seeds) to avoid any unwanted pesticide residues.

To grow a full tray (33cm x 22cm) of wheat grass you will need:

500g organic wheat grass seeds (grains)

1 litre peat-free, organic compost

1 seed tray (approx. 33cm x 22cm)

First soak the seeds in cold water overnight or for approximately 8 hours to allow them to germinate. Then rinse well in a colander or sieve using clean water. Gently mix the grains with the compost and spread evenly inside your tray.

Keep your tray of wheat grass in a warm, bright place away from direct sunlight and ensure it is evenly watered using a can with a fine rose, or misting spray. In the first few days, the seeds will not need a lot of water but should be kept moist. Once the roots have grown and plenty of green shoots have started to appear, water thoroughly and evenly every day.

Your wheat grass is ready to harvest after approximately 10 days of growth when the blades begin to 'split' – this is when the seed sends out a second shoot alongside the first giving the appearance of a split leaf, typically when the shoot is around 12–15cm high. Use scissors to snip the deep green grass at the bottom of the shoots and add them direct to your juicer. Placing a wedge of apple, carrot or another relatively hard ingredient on top of the grass in the juicing tube will help to push the shoots through. The cut wheat grass will keep for up to a week in a cool, damp bag (e.g. in the fridge), but it has most nutrients directly after cutting. Keep watering for a second crop, but after a couple of weeks the grass takes on a slightly bitter taste and you are better off starting the process again.

Spirulina – 1

This ancient blue-green alga is now cultivated in freshwater ponds to create a sustainable and planet-friendly form of protein, rich in essential amino acids and minerals – notably calcium and iron. It is also an excellent source of chlorophyll, B vitamins, vitamin E and zinc. One of the richest sources of plant protein, spirulina is every vegan and vegetarian's best friend. Slightly milder than chlorella, I find it works well in breakfast juices to add a powerful hit of protein.

Barley grass – 2

A relatively new 'green food', tender young barley leaves are harvested, dried and powdered to create a good source of soluble dietary fibre, chlorophyll and magnesium. Barley grass powder also adds an alkalising greenness to juice blends and can be used in a similar way to wheat grass (you can even sprout your own using the same method, see page 78). Barley grass is reputedly easier for the system to process than wheat grass.

Chlorella – 3

This powerful, extremely strong tasting, dark green plant is cultivated in freshwater pools and is a potent mix of protein, vitamins, minerals and chlorophyll. It is an absolute must-have super food for vegetarians and vegans, or for anyone on a restricted diet, because it is rich in B vitamins, vitamin E, absorbable iron, zinc and calcium.

Hemp – 4

Hemp has been harvested for thousands of years and is one of the world's most versatile plants. Its seeds are a rich source of protein, minerals and Omega-3 essential fatty acids. Dried and milled into a fine flour, this powder makes an excellent addition to juices, transforming them into protein-rich shakes. An added benefit is that this potent powder has much of the goodness without the same strong 'green' taste of other super-food additions, such as chlorella or spirulina.

Acai powder – 5

The acai is a grape-like purple berry from a species of palm tree. It has become one of the most famous new super foods and has travelled the globe from its native Brazil. Long used by indigenous people in the Amazon rainforest, it is highly prized for its distinctive taste and deep purple colour. A rich source of antioxidants, Omega-3 essential fatty acids, iron, calcium and amino acids, in powdered form acai works especially well blended into juices and smoothies, or mixed into homemade raw energy bars. Though nutritionally useful, it has been subject to quite a few false claims regarding weight loss and other super-strength health powers. Acai is an interesting food supplement, not necessarily a wonder berry (its antioxidant levels are actually less than those of pomegranate, grape, blueberry and black cherry juice) but useful nonetheless.

− 3 −

Juicing
therapy
& juice
cures

Food has been used to heal the sick for centuries and many of us will know the words of Hippocrates, the 'father' of medicine: 'Let food be your medicine, and your medicine be your food.' As modern day examples, figs and prunes still make excellent laxatives; cabbage juice helps to soothe peptic ulcers; cucumbers and fennel are wonderful natural diuretics. It's this therapeutic – as well as nutritious – potential that has led many naturopaths to use certain foods as a curative therapy.

To a great extent we are what we eat. The food we put into our bodies determines the health of every single cell. This is why it is so important to eat food that is fresh and alive in order to build healthy tissues and organs and to keep the system working properly. Consuming raw, natural, uncooked food is the key to building and maintaining health, which is why fresh juices are one of the best ways to keep well. If we feed our bodies with the maximum amount of a range of nutrients and the minimum of toxins, we can go a long way to ensuring a long and healthy life. Any health gain takes time and effort and a willingness to change. If you think about it, we are today what we ate yesterday, and only you can change that.

Fruits are revitalisers and cleansers and help to keep the channels of elimination functioning properly, while vegetables, in addition to being cleansing and restorative, also contain many of the building blocks of life. These amazing plants underpin the natural process of the body cleansing, restoring and healing itself, which is why naturopaths recommend a diet that contains raw fruit and vegetables for fitness, health and longevity. The Swiss physician and naturopath, Dr Bircher-Benner, famous for developing muesli and founding the Bircher-Benner Clinic, said that 'nothing more therapeutic exists on Earth than green juices'. He and Dr Max Gerson, practising in the United States, devised treatment programmes that involved the consumption of large quantities of fresh juice. The startling results both doctors achieved for their patients should convince anyone of the healing power of eating raw vegetables and fruit.

Fasting

Fasting is one of the oldest forms of natural health cure; references to fasting are made in the Bible and other ancient spiritual tomes. A period of abstinence from food gives a boost to the physical body, and it also helps to cleanse and renew the spirit. Many religious fasts were – and still are – undertaken for this reason because they help devotees to reach new levels of spiritual awareness and overcome the desires of the flesh. Dr Otto Buchinger, who developed the Buchinger method of fasting, comments: 'The world of prayer, in fact religions generally, and the world of fasting are closely related. Indeed, each one promotes the other.' Fasting is certainly an all-embracing treatment affecting body and soul simultaneously. The contemporary equivalent we may be more familiar with is the 5:2 diet – five days of eating and essentially two days of fasting per week – which is intended to promote health as well as weight loss. Practised in conjunction with eating plenty of raw food, fasting can be very powerful indeed. It is one of the most ancient forms of healing and traditionally has been used to cure a wide range of illnesses such as asthma, bronchitis, rheumatism, obesity, migraine, acne, liver problems, constipation, gallstones and even cancerous tumours.

The principle of fasting is very simple: restoration or self-healing of the body through cleansing. We have the ability to detoxify our systems, but in today's world we are bombarded with toxins – from environmental pollutants and agricultural chemicals to rancid, damaged fats and food additives. Unless these poisons are eliminated, they can overload the liver, kidneys, lungs, skin and colon. Some toxins may lodge themselves within our cells and tissues and eventually cause disease. When the body does not have to use its energy for digesting and processing of food, it is better able to self-heal, eliminate poisons more easily and rebalance its internal chemistry. The vital force within us can heal and protect, but only if we do not overburden our digestive and eliminative system with treated or processed foods and we avoid those external factors that deplete our natural vitality, such as stress, bad living and pollution. Fasting gives the body time to use its latent curative powers to rejuvenate body, mind and spirit.

Many respected practitioners of natural healthcare incorporate a period of abstinence from food in their treatments. Fasting specialist Dr Werner Zabel stated that 'hardly any other healing method reaches so deeply into a sick body as fasting'. Dr Max Gerson returned the ancient principles of fasting to popular use as part of the Gerson Therapy programme, a powerful form of cancer treatment based on raw food and juices. Inspired by the work of Gerson, the American 'Juiceman' Jay Kordich cured himself of a serious illness by drinking 13 glasses of carrot and apple juice every day for two years. That was 40 years ago, and since then he has dedicated his life to spreading the word about the wonders of juicing and fasting. More recent examples include the energetic 'wellness specialist' Joe Cross, Australian star of the juicing documentary *Fat, Sick and Nearly Dead*, which aptly charts his progress from being just that – to the ultimate green-juice crusader. Other well-known and respected champion juicers include Jason Vale (the Juice Master), who focuses on weight loss as well as health gain, and naturopath and all-round wellbeing guru Michael van Straten.

Fasting can be used both as a treatment of chronic diseases and as a preventative therapy. It is of course far better to prevent illness than to find a cure once it has taken hold. When animals get sick or ill, they stop eating until they begin to feel better again. We can learn a lot from this basic instinct. Fasting gives the body the time it needs to flush out the backlog of toxins. During a short fast the body is able to cleanse, purify and rebuild itself. Longer fasts, of more than a few days, can result in deep cleansing at tissue level where accumulated toxins and wastes have built up over long periods. Taken up with the daily process of digestion, assimilation and elimination, the body doesn't have the energy to remove toxins at this deeper level. (My eBook *Quick Guide to Detox* looks in depth at this subject, if you want to read more – details at the back of this book.)

The longest juice-only fast I have undertaken was ten days, combined with a daily visit to a naturopath. Once past the first couple of days of craving something to crunch, I got completely into the juice-only routine, and by the end of my routine I felt more energised and my skin looked more radiant than I could possibly have imagined. That was many years ago and now I find the daily pressures of running five children, a farm and international businesses make it much harder to take such dedicated time-out. However, I do still carry out shorter juice-fasts, such as the ones outlined on pages 89–93, always to great personal benefit.

It may help to view fasting as a day off from normal bodily processes, in which the body can cleanse, purify and resurrect itself – and we all need the occasional day off. Fasting is both appealing and challenging and can be a time for looking inward and assessing possible life changes. It gives us an opportunity to assess where we are and what we want to achieve. In a nutshell, fasting offers the chance to cleanse the inner psyche as well as the outer physique – and juice-fasting offers a very quick and easy way.

Juice-fasting

Strictly speaking, a fast means complete abstinence from food, but water may be drunk freely. Juices have the advantage over water in that not only do they flush out the system, they also nurture and strengthen the body with vitality and nutrients. Short juice-fasts – up to three days – are a wonderful way to rid the body of toxins and boost the eliminative system. Juice-fasts stimulate the whole metabolic process: excess weight falls off, your skin becomes clearer, your

hair shines and your eyes brighten while the intestines are cleansed and essential organs release stored-up waste.

By drinking fresh juices you bypass the part of the digestive process that separates liquid from bulk, thus making digestion less taxing on the body as a whole. At the same time you are absorbing all you need in terms of life-giving enzymes and nutrients in just a few minutes. Restricting your intake to an abundance of raw, uncooked foods will instantly make you feel more refreshed and energised. Freshly made juices contain around 95 per cent of the food value of whole fruit and vegetables and this package of nutrients, enzymes and vitality is instantly released into the body through the bloodstream. The road to health and vitality begins with cleansing and regenerating your whole body – and juice-fasting can form a first step in that process.

Who can juice-fast?

Juice-fasting is, for the overwhelming majority of us, completely harmless and anyone who wants better health, more energy and a longer lifespan can have a go. That said, those with chronic conditions, such as diabetes, heart disease, liver disease or cancer, as well as the elderly and pregnant women, should always consult their doctor before undertaking a fast. Most healthy people can safely fast for between one and three days. But if you have any worries at all then speak to your doctor or an experienced practitioner first.

The inner-cleansing juice diet

Just as it sounds, inner cleansing means a focus on removing unwanted waste matter from the body. One of the very best ways to cleanse is by fasting, either on water alone or on juices. Juices are nature's cleansers and either on their own or combined with solid food they make a huge difference to how we look and feel. This chapter provides recipe ideas for juice-fasting and a healthy eating plan for an all-round cleansing (detox) diet.

Inner cleansing through detoxification has been practised for thousands of years, which definitely rules it out as being the latest health fad. Toxins are nothing new either; they have been around for as long as fasting and are formed as natural by-products of the digestive processes, such as uric acid, lactic acid and adrenalin. The theory is that if the body is overburdened with waste products it cannot efficiently eliminate these natural toxins – let alone deal with all the artificial toxins and pollutants we accumulate from chemicals and other environmental hazards. The excess wastes and impurities of today's world build up in our bodies, resulting in slow metabolism, fatigue, tired or blemished skin, dull hair and eyes and general malaise. All these signs tell us that we need to inner cleanse. A healthy system can cope with a certain amount of toxic material, but bombard it with an overload of salt, sugar, alcohol, cigarette smoke, stress, worry, allergens, frustration, anger or chemicals, coupled with a lack of exercise and bad diet – it is scarcely surprising if our bodies start to complain and crumble.

An inner-cleansing juice diet helps to:

- rid the body of accumulated wastes by releasing them from the cells and tissues

- flush waste products out through the kidneys, liver, lungs, skin and colon

- restore a healthy pH balance

- strengthen the blood and immune systems

- give the body a rest

The outward signs of an inner cleanse are glowing skin, shiny hair, sparkling eyes, vitality, zest and much more. Common ailments, such as allergies, mood swings, headaches and depression, can all be improved, too. Sceptics should try it to believe it!

For many of us, unwelcome changes in our physical appearance can be a prime motivator for rethinking our diet, particularly in the respect of weight gain and cellulite. Neither of these represents an inevitable part of ageing and inner cleansing can really help to shift both kilos and these unsightly fatty deposits.

Fresh juices are helpful for any weight-loss programme since they are virtually fat-free and relatively low in calories, while also being high in energising nutrients. For example, a 200ml glass of fruit juice contains about 100 calories, and the same amount of vegetable juice contains even less than that. Drinking juices also helps curb the appetite and speeds up the metabolism. Any plan of healthy eating will tend to 'normalise' the whole system and bring us to our personal optimum weight.

A short juice-fast can be a step in the right direction, but any long-term weight loss requires permanent changes in the way we view our food and drink, as well as how we eat and live.

Cellulite is really a build-up of unwanted cell debris (toxins) in the fat cells. Nature is wise and puts toxins in the least harmful areas, away from vital organs and tissues such as our heart and brain. Fat cells are a relatively safe place to dump toxins, but cellulite is still a sign that the body could do with a bit of a detox. Banishing cellulite for good can be an ongoing campaign in which juice-fasts play a valuable role.

How often should we juice-fast?

This really depends on what you can manage individually and what commitments and lifestyle you have. At the very least, though, most healthy people can manage a one-day juice-fast a week and this is what the American 'Juiceman' Jay Kordich recommends. Longer fasts of three days can be carried out monthly or so. The idea behind any inner-cleansing diet is also educational. Eventually your body will be re-educated into new and healthier ways of eating and a healthier lifestyle. Read about this in more detail in my ebook *Liz Earle's Quick Guide to Detox*.

One-day juice fast

The most powerful juice-fast is a fruit-based one, as these juices (especially citrus) are considered to be stronger intestinal cleansers than vegetable juices. However, a pure fruit juice-fast also has the potential to leave you feeling a bit rough. Ideally, try to drink a mix of fruit and vegetable juices throughout the day, plus plenty of filtered or bottled water and herb teas if desired.

Daily elements of a juice-fast:

- Diet: fresh juices, bottled or filtered water, herb teas

- Internal cleansing: enemas (optional), psyllium husks

- External cleansing: Epsom salts, sauna, steam bath, skin brushing, showers

- Exercise: walking, swimming, cycling, yoga, breathing, T'ai chi, stretch rebounding

- Rest: peace, prayer, meditation

Getting ready

- It is important to prepare mentally, which means getting into a positive frame of mind so that you can complete the fast.

- Set aside a day when you can relax and rest as much as possible as this will benefit your whole system. You may be lucky enough to be able to book a massage or fit in a steam or sauna session that day, to assist with the cleansing process. At the very least, try and choose a day when the children are at school, or being looked after by others preferably when your schedule is quieter and you can actually manage a day without having to respond to every single text or email (increasingly difficult!).

- Make sure you have all the ingredients you will need for the day ahead – including plenty of fresh fruit and vegetables, herb teas, etc. and optional extras such as a dry skin brush, Epsom salts or an enema kit.

- Try to keep as quiet and peaceful as possible, avoiding TV and computer screens as well as busy places and stressful situations (a daily commute, for example). Inner cleansing can also be a time to contemplate – and peace and quiet will help with this process.

- Prepare your digestive system the day (or evening) before the fast. This could be a mono-fruit day (i.e. eating one type of fruit only) or just eating lightly, avoiding meat, fish, eggs, dairy produce and wheat. If you are a coffee-addict, you may experience a caffeine-withdrawal headache on a fast day. If this does happen, you can either wean yourself off coffee during the week before, gradually cutting down a cup each day until you are at zero, or simply allow yourself one small cup of black coffee during the day to keep the headaches at bay (which, frankly, is what I do when I'm feeling particularly stressed).

Shopping list:

4 apples

8 carrots

¼ cucumber

1 celery stick

2 oranges

1 lemon

largish lump of fresh ginger root

pure, filtered water

selection of herb teas

Optional

vegetable fibre or natural-bristle body brush

enema kit – these come with instructions (entirely optional!)

1–2kg Epsom salts

psyllium husks or linseeds

During the day try to drink about 1–2 litres of filtered or bottled water as well as the juices to help flush toxins out of the system.

Three juices per day will probably be enough to start with since they are powerful internal cleansers and can stir up the elimination process of waste matter more quickly than you can comfortably eliminate. You can dilute juices with water if you feel they may be too strong. If you want to have more than three juices a day, psyllium husks or Epsom salt baths will really help with elimination *(see pages 94–95 for details)*.

Any detox programme is greatly enhanced if you also take some light exercise such as yoga, walking or breathing exercises, but remember not to overdo it, since the body may need extra energy for processing released waste matter and you could feel slightly weak or faint if you don't take it easy. Relaxation is an important part of inner-cleansing or detox diets. This is a perfect time to pamper yourself – book a massage, sauna or facial, for example. Or give yourself an at-home spa including a facial massage, manicure and pedicure. You could use the time to read, write letters, knit, draw, meditate or listen to music.

On rising	A glass of hot water with a squeeze of lemon juice and a slice of ginger root to help cleanse the intestines and restore the pH balance. Body brush (see page 94), shower, make time for a little light exercise, such as stretching, yoga, Pilates-style core strengthening exercises or simple breathing exercises
Breakfast	250ml glass of apple, orange and ginger juice
Mid-Morning	250ml glass of water or herb tea, more if you like
Lunch	250ml glass of carrot and apple juice, with a dessertspoonful of powdered wheat grass, chlorella or spirulina (see pages 80–81)
Afternoon	250ml glass of water or herb tea, more if you like
Supper	250ml glass of carrot, celery and cucumber juice
Evening	250ml glass of water or herb tea

Three-day juice fast

Follow the guidelines for the one-day juice-fast for three consecutive days. You can choose different juices for each 'meal' from the recipes in chapters 4–7, or make up your own. The longer you fast, the greater the depth of cleansing – i.e. the body has more time in which to surrender its toxins for clearing and to rebuild worn and damaged tissues. None of the juice recipes are set in stone – they can be very much adapted to take into account personal preference, seasonality of produce, etc. The most important part of the process is Me-time. Personally, I find it impossible to carry out a three-day juice-fast if I'm also expected to cook for a hungry husband or the rest of the family, work under pressure or be in any way social – so these three-day wonders really do require a bit of scheduling and diary management.

The first day is always the hardest because the body needs time to adapt to going without food and you may feel a little hungry. But Don't Panic!! The rewards are great, the hunger-pangs will pass and you will have more energy and clarity of mind after fasting than you might have believed possible. During a longer fast, more toxins are removed from the cells and you may feel slightly unwell as the toxins are released into the system for clearing. Naturopaths may recommend including enemas, Epsom salt baths or psyllium husks during three-day fasts to help with elimination (see pages 94–95). Caffeine enemas are reputed to be especially good at stimulating the liver and helping it to detoxify through the bowel. Again, these elements are optional and although many people find them beneficial they are by no means compulsory.

Optional extras

These extras are by no means essential to cleansing and detoxification, but they can certainly help eliminate toxins from the body.

Years of bad eating habits coupled with sluggish elimination organs can lead to a build-up of impacted waste matter in the bowel and lower intestines, which is particularly hard to shift through juicing alone. These optional extras are designed to thoroughly cleanse and stimulate our organs for detoxification – in particular, the skin and the bowel. However, it is important to consult your own doctor or healthcare practitioner first if you are at all unsure about any of the following aids to elimination.

Psyllium husks

These are the seeds of the plantain and are a form of natural fibre unsurpassed in their ability to remove sticky mucus and toxins from the bowel. Psyllium husks are a well-known remedy for ulcers and constipation, they help stimulate urine flow, bowel movements and make a great addition to any detox or inner-cleansing diet. The husks are available from most health-food outlets either as a loose powder or in capsules that can be opened and sprinkled into juices in a handy pre-measured dose. The important thing is to ensure that you drink at least one glass of water per three or four capsules or teaspoon of husks. This is because they swell up with water to form a bulky jelly-like mass that absorbs toxins and carries them out of the body. A word of advice: if you add psyllium husks to a juice don't forget to drink it immediately – as they soon swell up and expand to create an unappetising (but healthy!) sludge in the glass.

Linseeds

Linseeds are rich in fibre and essential fatty acids and can be used instead of psyllium husks (their action is slightly gentler as they don't swell to the same extent). Take one dessertspoonful of linseeds two or three times daily with one of your juices or a little plain, organic, live yogurt, or sprinkle them on soups and salads. For the seeds to work effectively, it is important that you drink at least 150ml of water or juice per dessertspoonful of seeds.

Dry skin body brushing

Brushing your skin all over with a dry bristle brush may sound a little odd, but it is a great way to stimulate the lymphatic system and it helps clear and revitalise the skin. Body brushes can be found in most chemists and health-food stores, and the best kind are made with vegetable bristles and have long handles so you can reach your back easily.

Use a brush on dry skin, brushing the body in brisk sweeps towards the lower abdomen. You always begin at your feet and move upwards until you reach your abdomen, then begin to brush down from your neck and shoulders. Brush towards the heart and avoid sensitive or broken skin.

Epsom salts baths

Epsom salts are made from magnesium sulphate and this old-fashioned, time-tested remedy helps draw impurities from the skin. The salts are available from chemists and some health-food stores.

A fair quantity is required for each bath – add about a kilo of salts to a deep, hot bath, and then soak for 15–20 minutes. When you get out, wrap yourself in a warm dressing gown or comfy clothes, get into bed and sweat, sweat, sweat! As you perspire, toxins will continue to be released through the skin. Just make sure you replenish lost moisture by drinking at least one large glass of pure water. Definitely one of my favourite at-home health and beauty treatments – simple but effective.

Enemas

A form of home colonic irrigation; you can find enema kits in good health shops and chemists or from naturopathic suppliers online. They come with instructions and can be a helpful addition to an inner-cleansing regime, by flushing the lower bowel with pure, clean water. Colonic irrigation, conducted by an experienced and qualified practitioner, can also be a useful internal cleansing treatment.

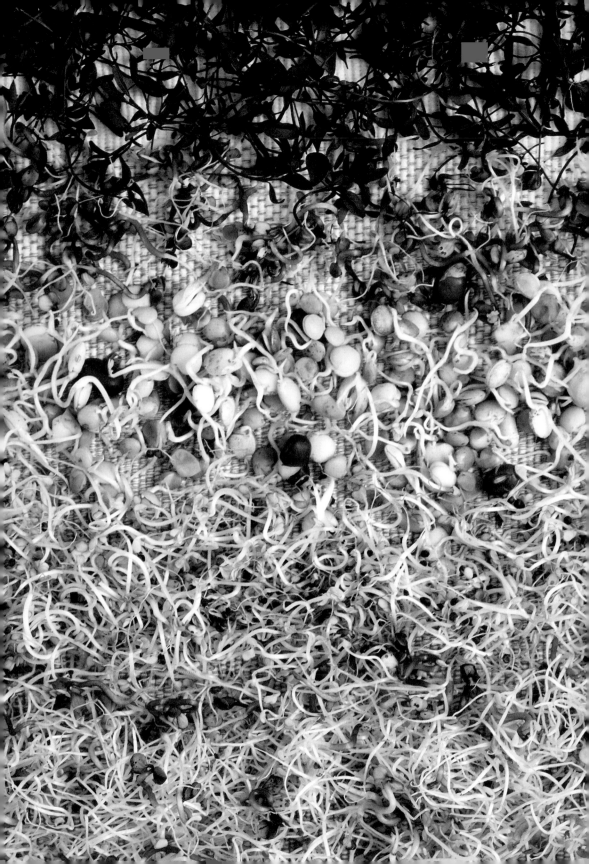

– 4 –

Juicing
for weight
loss

Juicing has a huge part to play in helping with weight loss and there are a number of ways it can do this, mainly in supporting two systems in the body – digestion and elimination, but also by increasing energy levels and reducing intake of foods that may inhibit weight loss. I recommend that before you begin your weight-loss regime you undertake a two-day mini juice-fast to help kick-start the process – it really helps.

There are strong reasons for including juicing as part of a weight-reduction programme. First, because unwanted cellular waste matter (toxins) are removed by drinking raw juices, excess weight is also reduced since many toxins are stored in fat cells. Second, by ingesting more sulphur-rich vegetables we are supporting the liver which is responsible for metabolising everything we eat or are exposed to in the environment. Even though we may not be able to control what we are exposed to, we can increase our intake of sulphur-rich food to help the detoxification process. Sulphur-rich vegetables include: asparagus, garlic, leeks, onions and the cruciferous (meaning cabbage-like) vegetables (broccoli, Brussels sprouts, kale and cabbage). Alfalfa, chicory and other 'bitter' foods are also excellent for detoxification since they help stimulate bile activity, the liquid substance that helps break down fat for easier digestion within the body.

It is important to lose weight in a slow and controlled manner because, as excess weight is lost, the liver must detoxify the toxins that were stored in the fat cells. This process in turn can contribute to fatigue and headaches since it diverts energy from other vital daily body functions, together with lethargy, caused by a lower intake of calories, and withdrawal symptoms.

Reducing our intake of processed foods and increasing the amount of low-calorie, fibre-rich fruit and vegetable juices we consume doesn't just cleanse our systems; the fabulous nutrients juices contain also support our bodies whilst weight is being lost. Juicing puts very little stress on the digestive system and helps suppress hunger pangs, so we're less tempted to reach for unhealthy foods that will only increase our waistlines... Remember, though, while juices may be fat-free they do contain calories, a fact you need to take into account when balancing your daily intake of food. Fruit juices are high in sugar, and if sugar is not burnt off it will turn to fat, so focus more on replacing meals with a filling vegetable juice, which will leave you feeling satisfied without as many calories. And don't forget to drink plenty of water throughout the day. Fibre, too, helps with satiety, so you may want to include a sprinkling of psyllium husks into your juices from time to time (see page 94).

The aim here is to lose fat and not muscle, and therefore it's important to ensure you still eat enough protein throughout the day to repair and rebuild muscle. So, if your meal-replacement juice doesn't include protein, make sure the other meals do. Fish (especially oily varieties rich in beneficial Omega-3 essential fatty acids), grilled chicken and other lean meats, together with eggs and vegetarian tofu are all good protein choices.

The fact that juicing naturally gives us more energy (especially if you try the energy juice recipes in chapter 7) makes us more inclined to exercise, thereby improving our chances of achieving quick, successful weight loss. Once you see the benefits you won't look back.

These are some of my personal favourites when it comes to shedding a few pounds. I use each of these delicious, healthy juices as an occasional meal replacement, basing my choice on the seasonality of the ingredients and what takes my mood. All are fabulously tasty and a treat in their own right too.

Luscious Lean Leek

There is no doubt that leek juice is an acquired taste so do not add too much the first time you try this! Leeks are very rich in sulphur, and therefore great for detoxing, and hugely strong on flavour (they will make your eyes water too)! Be sure to juice them with something sweet to counteract the strong flavour. Coriander is rich in vitamins and minerals, and adds a wonderful earthy flavour to this juice.

¼ small leek (including the upper green leaves)

1 lime

1 large tomato

1 small handful coriander (use fresh parsley if you prefer the flavour, as I do)

2 carrots

Juice all the ingredients and stir well before serving.

Spicy Spears

Asparagus contains glutathione, a potent antioxidant, well known for its detoxifying properties as well as being a natural diuretic and a good source of fibre, iron, and vitamins A (in the form of beta-carotene), C, E and K. Juicing it with apples and cinnamon gives a tasty, sweet juice. The addition of cinnamon is not just for taste – it is a spice that is important in helping to control blood sugar levels and sugar cravings. Fabulously zingy – whilst the cinnamon helps keep the sweet-tooth munchies at bay.

8 asparagus spears

2 apples

1 large pinch ground cinnamon

Juice the asparagus and apples and then stir in the ground cinnamon before serving.

Enzyme Attack

The delicious buttery consistency and taste of papaya is not lost when juicing the fruit. Papaya contains papain, an enzyme that helps to digest protein, as well as high levels of vitamin C and beta-carotene. Here it is teamed with pineapple, another tropical, vitamin C-rich fruit that contains bromelain, another protein-digesting enzyme. Pineapple is also thought to help reduce inflammation.

1 papaya, peeled and seeds removed

1 x 3cm thick slice fresh pineapple, skin removed, plus extra to decorate

½ lime

1 large handful mint leaves

Juice all the ingredients, mix well and serve over ice with a slice of pineapple.

A juicy sweet treat.

Summer Slimmer

Strawberries help to increase the body's production of a hormone that stimulates our metabolism and may act to curb our appetite. Anthocyanins, a chemical constituent of strawberries and other red berries, including grapes, stimulate the hormone adiponectin, which is produced by fat cells – and, usefully, this hormone stimulates fat burning. The addition of cabbage in this juice adds important sulphur for liver support, but does not detract from the summery strawberry flavour. Extremely refreshing and a natural appetite-quencher.

12–14 strawberries

1/5 small Savoy cabbage, roughly chopped

1 small handful fresh mint leaves

Juice all the ingredients, mix well and serve immediately.

1. The Green Dream Cleaning Machine
2. Watercress Wonder
3. Kale and Hearty

The Green Dream Cleaning Machine

This juice is full of chlorophyll and rich in antioxidants, so important for cleansing and fighting damaging free radicals, but also very filling and nutritious. Swiss chard leaves contain at least 13 different antioxidants, plus a flavonoid called syringic acid, which has been shown to inhibit the activity of an enzyme that breaks down simple sugars, making this vegetable a great support for blood sugar control, very important when you are trying to control weight. Just look at these ingredients! You can't help but enjoy drinking this super-slimming green genie.

1 carrot

$^1/_5$ cucumber

1 small bunch parsley

1 small handful spinach

1 small handful Swiss chard

1 celery stick

1 lime

Juice all the ingredients, mix together and serve immediately.

Watercress Wonder

Watercress is a fantastic ingredient for juicing, not only for its great flavour, but because it's rich in many vitamins – A (in the form of beta-carotene), C, E and K – and excellent in aiding calcium intake. Juiced with sulphur-rich asparagus, tart green apples, pineapple and cucumber it makes a light, fresh tangy juice. The bromelain contained in pineapple is an enzyme that assists in digestion by helping to break down proteins. This juice also makes a deliciously healthy appetiser. A truly delicious combo!

1 large handful watercress

4 asparagus spears

1 green apple

1 x 2cm thick slice fresh pineapple, skin removed

¼ cucumber

Juice all the ingredients, mix well and serve immediately.

Kale and Hearty

This juice is rich in sulphur, which is known to support the liver – kale contains the compound sulforaphane, while beetroot and parsley are great liver cleansers too. The addition of psyllium husks gives additional fibre to help clean out the intestines and keep the body systems working at optimal levels – this recipe works especially well as a meal-replacement juice.

2 handfuls kale

1 medium beetroot

1 large handful parsley

2 celery sticks

1 lemon, roughly peeled to remove the yellow zest, but keep the pith

1 capsule psyllium husk

Juice the vegetables and lemon and then open the psyllium husk capsule and stir into the juice before serving. Drink immediately (before the psyllium husks solidify!).

Cool Cabbage

It is thought that the various types of cabbage (red, green, Savoy, etc.) contain different patterns of glucosinolates, so eating a variety of these vegetables gives us the broadest range of benefits. The rich red colour of red cabbage reflects its concentration of nutrients, including the amino acid glutamine, which is known to support the digestive tract. As with all cabbage juice, the flavour is quite strong, so juicing with cooling cucumber and citrusy lemon is a perfect match. Sip slowly, savouring each mouthful – this juice makes an excellent (super healthy) meal-replacement drink.

¼ cucumber

1 carrot

1 stick celery

1 small wedge red cabbage

¼ lemon

1cm piece fresh ginger root, peeled

Juice all the ingredients, mix well and serve immediately.

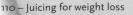

– 5 –

Juicing for better skin

The skin is a remarkable, complex organ that accurately reflects our overall health – it's also the largest organ of the body. Not only is our skin exposed to damage or disease from external factors, but also it reflects our internal conditions and emotions, such as when we sweat or blush. So, a clear, radiant-looking skin is a visible indication that all the other systems in the body are in good order too.

To act as a protective layer, our skin needs to be nourished from within. Unstable molecules known as free radicals damage skin cells and are responsible for many of the signs of ageing. By ensuring our diet includes plenty of antioxidant nutrients such as vitamins A (in the form of beta-carotene), C and E, together with the minerals zinc and selenium, we can prevent damage caused by free radicals. Importantly, none of these vitamins or minerals work in isolation; they support each other and work synergistically, so eating a variety of healthy foods means we're getting the full range of mutually beneficial nutrients.

Another antioxidant, the coenzyme Q10 (Co-Q10), has a vital role in helping to protect cells as it recycles vitamin E. Co-Q10 is found in all meat and fish (especially sardines), eggs, spinach, broccoli, alfalfa, potato, wheatgerm, rice bran and most beans, nuts and seeds. It's a real power-house when it comes to saving our skin from premature ageing, and the recipes for green juices in this section are especially rich in it.

Anthocyanins are powerful antioxidants from the flavonoid family – these are present in deep-coloured fruits and vegetables, such as strawberries, blueberries, black grapes and Swiss chard. To ensure you are getting a healthy supply, make sure your juices are full of naturally colourful foods.

Two types of essential fats (known as essential fatty acids – EFAs) also contribute to healthy skin: omega-3 and omega-6. Each cell membrane in the body is partly composed of essential fats, and our skin is made up of these cells. EFAs help to keep the membranes soft and smooth, which is important in controlling what passes in and out of the cells. EFAs also help reduce inflammation, maintain good blood flow and hormone balance, and much more that is key to everyday health. The following oils are all readily available so including these in our juices every day, is a great step towards radiant, glowing skin.

Oil	Vitamin E (per 100g)	Omega-3*	Omega-6*
Avocado	2mg	–	10%
Chia seed	–	30%	40%
Flax seed	35mg	58%	14%
Hemp seed	90mg	20%	60%
Olive	5.10mg	–	8%
Rapeseed	22.21mg	7%	30%

* Fatty acid profiles of all natural oils will vary depending on the strain, location, latitude and weather conditions of the year the plants were grown

The technical description for ageing is 'a progressive accumulation of damage to an organism over time, eventually leading to disease and death'. As far as our skin is concerned, research has revealed how Advanced Glycation End products (funnily enough, known as AGEs) are a major factor in ageing. As we age, our structural skin proteins are damaged by something called glycation, which occurs when sugar reacts with amino acids (protein). AGEs, a complex group of compounds that form during this process, have been implicated in a number of diabetes- and age-related diseases. More recent research is focusing on the role of AGEs in skin wrinkling and general ageing.

There are two primary sources of AGEs. The first is the food we eat and the way we cook it – the browning of food is achieved by heating it (for example, cooking a steak) or by cooking sugars with proteins (such as making a rich stew or sauce) and in the process AGEs are formed. The second is through normal metabolism, where carbohydrates (both simple and complex) are absorbed by the body to affect blood sugar levels. Most of our blood sugar is used to provide energy to enable the body to function, but a small amount of the blood sugar is glycated to form AGEs. It might sound strange, but glycation is actually part of our normal metabolism and ageing process – it's just something we try to minimise to help keep ageing at bay. Ways to reduce the formation of AGEs include reducing our intake of sugar, eating vegetables and fruits raw (so here again, juices are ideal) or boiled or lightly steamed, limiting our intake of processed or 'browned' foods, and – that old beauty chestnut – drinking plenty of water.

The recipes on the following pages include some of my favourite beauty-boosting juices – great to sit alongside your botanical skincare regime!

Citrus Roots

This tangy and refreshing juice is rich in beta-carotene from the carrots, while the addition of potato makes it a great internal skin cleanser. The taste is sweet, but lemon grass and lime add an excellent tang. Chia oil is a valuable source of alpha lipoic acid, a powerful antioxidant that helps to encourage healthier skin cell function.

2 carrots

1 parsnip

½ medium potato

1 lemon grass stalk (peel off woody stem unless using a juicer with a high-power motor)

1 apple

½ lime

1 teaspoon chia oil

Juice the fruit and vegetables, then stir in the chia oil and serve.

Summer Mint

All the ingredients of a sunny summer in one glass. Cantaloupe melons are an excellent source of vitamins A (beta-carotene) and C, as well as potassium, niacin and vitamin B6. On top of that, the yield from one melon can make enough juice for the whole family! The cucumber is also an excellent source of potassium. The addition of strawberries and mint rounds off the great summery taste, and a teaspoon of avocado oil or flax seed oil will increase your intake of vitamin E.

$^1/_3$ cucumber

¼ cantaloupe melon, flesh removed as close to the skin as possible

8–10 strawberries

1 small handful mint, plus a sprig to decorate

1 teaspoon avocado or flax seed oil

Juice the cucumber, melon, strawberries and mint. Stir in the avocado oil and serve in an ice-filled glass topped with a sprig of mint.

Sprouting Greens

This is a seriously green juice – in colour and taste. If you choose only one skin-saving juice – I suggest you make it this one! Kale is a true skin super food, not only rich in vitamin K, but also highly prized amongst nutritionists for its omega-3 content and over 40 different flavonoids that make it both an antioxidant and anti-inflammatory. Broccoli sprouts have been shown to contain levels of sulforaphane 100 times higher than those found in the plant itself. Sulforaphane is a compound that improves the liver's ability to detoxify, an essential process for skin clarity and overall health.

4–5 handfuls kale

1 handful parsley

2 kiwi fruit, peeled

1 lime

1 handful broccoli sprouts

½ teaspoon spirulina

Juice all the fruit, vegetables and sprouts, and then stir in the spirulina before serving.

Skin Sunrise

Red peppers contain large amounts of vitamin C and A (beta-carotene), as well as B6 and magnesium, plus they taste really sweet, so are perfect for juicing. This recipe combines them with sweet carrots and an apple, with a touch of ginger to add a hint of spice.

3 carrots

1 apple

1 red pepper, seeds removed

2cm piece fresh ginger root, peeled

Juice all the ingredients, stir well and serve immediately.

Spiced Raspberries

This sweet and spicy juice is also very warming due to the inclusion of ginger, a root that has much culinary importance. Medicinally, ginger is valued for its unique phytochemicals and health-benefiting oils that give it antibacterial and anti-inflammatory properties. This juice is also a good source of sulphur, chlorophyll, vitamin E and anthocyanins – so an excellent all-round skin-saver. I recommend this juice when you feel your skin (and psyche) needs a bit of a pick-me-up.

2 large handfuls watercress

16–20 red grapes

1 handful raspberries

1cm piece fresh ginger root, peeled

Juice all the ingredients, stir well and serve immediately.

Melon Cocktail

Melons have a high water content, which is important for hydrating the skin, but they also contain valuable vitamins and minerals. Watermelon flesh is a great source of beta-carotene and vitamin C, while the seeds are rich in zinc and selenium, so it's an all-round great antioxidant. Cantaloupe is also rich in folic acid, an important nutrient for cell regeneration and helping to keep the wrinkles at bay.

3–4 broccoli florets

$1/5$ medium watermelon, peeled as close to the flesh as possible

¼ cantaloupe melon, peeled as close to the flesh as possible

1cm piece fresh ginger root, peeled

Juice all the ingredients, stir well and serve over ice.

Complexion Calmer

More of a smoothie with the addition of avocado. The calming and soothing ingredients such as cucumber and fennel can help to combat skin inflammation, such as eczema, psoriasis and rosacea. Skin-calming antioxidants and anti-inflammatory essential fatty acids also work well here, so try piercing a capsule of evening primrose or borage seed oil and adding it to the juice. This is another of my all-time favourites: a velvety green, smoothie-style juice.

> 1 apple
>
> 1 carrot
>
> ½ fennel bulb
>
> ¼ cucumber
>
> ½ avocado
>
> 1 capsule borage seed or evening primrose oil

Juice the apple, carrot, fennel and cucumber, in their entirety, in a juicer. Transfer the combined juices to a blender, add the avocado flesh and the contents of your chosen oil capsule, and whizz until smooth.

Greenie Genie

Alkalising green juices are especially beneficial for improving acne or problem skin. Go for ingredients such as asparagus, celery, parsley and watercress, and don't overload on high-sugar fruits. Carrot juice, rich in beta-carotene, is also a useful addition, but try to keep the juices mostly green. This is a deliciously light juice with a refreshing ginger tang. The grassiness of the green ingredients is slightly sweetened by the apples.

> 2 apples
>
> 2 carrots
>
> 2cm piece fresh ginger root, unpeeled
>
> 4 small asparagus spears
>
> 1 small handful parsley
>
> 1 small handful freshly cut wheat grass, or 1 level teaspoon powdered greens, such as wheat grass, chlorella or spirulina

Juice together all the ingredients, in their entirety, stirring in your chosen powdered greens (if using) just before serving.

Skin Soother

Cucumbers are not only very cooling, they are also rich in potassium, which helps give elasticity to the skin cells, whilst also being a great digestive aid. This is actually very important to ensure absorption of all the great nutrients in any juice. Adding blueberries increases our intake of vitamin C, an essential nutrient in the making of collagen, a protein that is essential for healthy skin and blood vessels. The fresh-tasting cos lettuce adds useful beta-carotene and vitamin K – both helpful for creating healthy skin cells. This juice has a fabulously clean taste.

1 cos lettuce

½ cucumber

1–2 handfuls blueberries

1 teaspoon flaxseed oil

Juice the cos, cucumber and berries and then stir in the flaxseed oil before serving.

Plumper Skin Perfecter

This is a juice for dry and mature skin. To tackle wrinkles, choose blueberries, blackberries, black grapes and dark cherries, all of which are rich in anthocyanins. (The vitamin C in the fruit is also useful, supporting collagen and elastin fibres.) Blend these, though, as juicing removes their skins, which contain polyphenols and resveratrol, two phytonutrients that have been linked to longevity because of their ability to slow down cell oxidisation. You can add essential fatty acids to the mix by piercing a capsule of evening primrose oil and a naturally sourced vitamin E capsule and adding the contents to the juice. Or simply add a dash of cold-pressed flaxseed, rapeseed, walnut or olive oil.

This is a fabulously pretty, subtly flavoured juice, and one that you can make if you don't have a juicer, as you could use freshly pressed apple juice from a carton.

2 apples

1 generous handful seedless black grapes

1 generous handful blueberries (about 30), blackberries or pitted dark cherries

½ tablespoon cold-pressed flaxseed, rapeseed, walnut or olive oil

Juice the apples, and then transfer to a blender. Add the grapes and your choice of berries or cherries and whizz until smooth. Stir in your chosen pure plant oil.

Virgin Mary

Well, you could add a touch of vodka to this delicious juice, but as it's so healthy it would be a shame to spoil it! Tomatoes are widely known for their antioxidant content, owing to their rich concentration of lycopene. Recent research shows an important connection between lycopene and bone health, as well as protection of the liver, kidneys and bloodstream. Lycopene is also a real skin saver as it helps repair skin damage resulting from inflammation and even reduces the severity of sunburn – which may be why tomatoes grow so well in hotter, Mediterranean climates. However, tomatoes are not for everyone, since these concentrated fruits of the nightshade family may be associated with joint pain or arthritis. Horseradish is a wonderful addition here as it is rich in sulphur to benefit both hair and skin.

10 medium tomatoes

2 celery sticks

1 garlic clove (optional)

¼ lime

1 small handful parsley

5mm slice fresh horseradish, peeled (optional)

Seasonings (any of the following)

Worcestershire sauce

Tabasco sauce (optional)

freshly milled black pepper

celery seeds

Juice the tomatoes, celery, garlic (if using), lime, parsley and horseradish (if using). Mix together, and then stir your choice of seasoning.

– 6 –

Juicing
for energy

Macronutrients – carbohydrates, proteins and fats – are the nutrients that provide calories, or energy. But before foods can give us this energy and vitality, hundreds of chemical reactions must take place, involving more than 30 vitamins and minerals, known as micronutrients. These micronutrients are the real key to unlocking the potential energy in our food, in the process known as metabolism. Metabolism is the sum of all the chemical reactions that take place in all the cells in the body, generating energy by converting the kilocalories in macronutrients into a more usable form. Because the body constantly needs energy, metabolism never stops, it simply adapts to changes in the environment, whether we're dancing the night away, or in the middle of a deep sleep. Juicing is a great way of increasing our intake of micronutrients needed for these chemical reactions. The B-Complex vitamins are often referred to as the energy vitamins. Foods rich in B vitamins include broccoli, asparagus, parsley, citrus fruits and most dark-green leafy vegetables. Other important micronutrients work synergistically to support this process and these include the minerals magnesium, calcium and manganese.

Powder power

Other valuable sources that contain nutrients to increase our energy levels have been identified by naturopaths and produced in a powder form that is easily assimilated by the body. Here are some of the most important and useful 'power powders' to add to your juices:

'Green' powders: Barley grass, wheat grass, chlorella and spirulina. Most of these are edible in their natural, unprocessed form, but as we're unlikely to add large handfuls of grass or algae to our lunch plate each day, taking them in the form of a powder in a juice is far more convenient. Cereal grasses and algae are hugely rich in chlorophyll, and provide phytonutrient (plant nutrient) antioxidants to help guard against free-radical damage. I mentioned previously that chlorophyll is a powerful blood cleanser and body builder; it also delivers a continuous energy transfusion into the bloodstream, replenishing and increasing the red blood cell (haemoglobin) count. Since haemoglobin carries oxygen to our cells, increasing haemoglobin in turn increases our levels of energy. Drinking a daily dose of these alkalising green powder-power juices is one of the fastest and easiest ways to help increase our energy levels.

Maca powder: Maca grows in central Peru and has been cultivated as a vegetable crop for at least 3,000 years. The plant is a relative of the radish and broccoli family with a nutty, slightly earthy taste. Maca contains many nutrients, including fatty acids and amino acids, is rich in vitamins B1, B2, C and E and many minerals, and has been classed as an 'adaptogen', which is the name given to an ingredient thought to help the body adapt to changes and stress. Including maca in the diet is claimed to increase energy and stamina, although scientific evidence is needed to back this up.

Powder (per 100g)	Protein	Iron	Zinc	Other nutrients
Barley grass	24g	10mg	1.9mg	Chlorophyll / magnesium / folic acid
Chlorella	61.3g	210mg	69.8mg	B vitamins / vitamin E
Spirulina	56.6g	82.7mg	3.3mg	Linolenic acid /chlorophyll / calcium
Wheat grass	21.5g	30mg	1.9mg	Potassium / magnesium
Maca	9.7g	15mg		Calcium / potassium

Ginseng powder

Chinese medicine has used the ginseng herb for its energy support and medicinal properties for thousands of years. The active ingredients in ginseng, known as 'ginsenocides', help to control hormone activity and the regulating mechanisms of our nerves. They are also thought to influence blood pressure and insulin production, and to increase metabolism. Ginseng may interact with certain prescribed or over-the-counter medicines, so do check with your GP or pharmacist before taking ginseng supplements.

Water power

Our energy levels are also affected by how hydrated we are. Water is responsible for transporting all the nutrients in the blood that we use for energy, as well as removing the build-up of waste that leads to fatigue. Water makes up more than 80 per cent of our blood, 75 per cent of our brain and 96 per cent of our liver. Although water itself does not produce energy, without it our cells could not receive energy from other nutrients. Drinking juices helps towards our daily water intake, but be sure you are getting enough – a recommended daily intake is around 1.5–2 litres.

The zingingly delicious juicing recipes on the following pages are all designed as potent energy-boosters. They are also excellent drinks for times of stress, over-work, convalesence or even (dare I say it)... hangovers.

Beety Energiser

Beetroot juice can be considered the emperor of all energisers, shown to increase stamina, boost brain power and even lower blood pressure. Here it is combined with the sweetness of apples, an antioxidant shot of carrots and the rejuvenating tang of fresh, zingy ginger to really get you back on your feet – fast!

This juice is dark, sweet and tangy. Serve with a sprig of mint and perhaps a slice of fresh lemon.

1 apple

2 carrots

3cm piece ginger root, unpeeled

1 beetroot

1 sprig fresh mint, leaves only

1 slice lemon, to serve (optional)

Juice all the ingredients. (When juicing herbs or leaves, don't forget to sandwich them between chunks of apple, carrot or beetroot to help flush them through the juicer.) Serve with a slice of lemon.

Battery Charge

This beautiful bright-orange-coloured juice makes a great way to start the day. Carrot juice contains high levels of beta-carotene, an antioxidant that can help oxygenate our blood, brain and body tissues. The addition of maca powder – rich in calcium, potassium and iron – also promotes oxygen transport around the body to help fight fatigue and tiredness.

3 carrots

1 garlic clove

1 orange, roughly peeled

½ teaspoon maca powder

Juice the carrots, garlic and orange, and then stir in the maca powder before serving.

Beetroot Beat-the-Blues

The ability of beetroot juice to lower blood pressure has been known for a number of years, but recent studies have also shown it to be helpful in increasing the efficient uptake of oxygen – vital during exercise – leading to far more stamina and staying power. This tasty red vegetable is also rich in magnesium, which may help to ease muscle tension, stress and anxiety. Juice it with sharp citrus fruits to soften the earthy flavour, and a little ginger to give a bit of zing!

1 orange, roughly peeled

1 small handful blueberries

2–3 medium beetroots

2cm piece fresh ginger root, peeled

½ teaspoon chlorella powder

Juice the fruit and vegetables, and then stir in the chlorella powder. Serve poured over ice.

Parsley Punch

Parsley is related to celery and is often overlooked as merely a garnish. It is a wonderful herb, rich in vitamins C, K and A, as well as folic acid, iron, copper and potassium; the rich flavonoids it contains also function as antioxidants. Juicing parsley with sweet apple, carrot and celery gives a clean, green, fresh-tasting juice. Stir in your favourite green powder for an extra hit of chlorophyll.

> 1 apple
>
> 1 carrot
>
> 2 celery sticks
>
> 1 large handful parsley
>
> ½ teaspoon wheat grass powder

Juice the apple and vegetables, stir in the wheat grass powder and serve.

Clean and Green

This juice tastes really clean and fresh, and the addition of grapefruit gives a delicious citrus sweetness. Spinach, being a great source of chlorophyll as well as vitamins C, E and K, beta-carotene, folic acid and calcium, is known to be a great health restorer. Recent research has also found that spinach contains more than a dozen different flavonoid compounds that function as anti-inflammatory and anti-cancer agents.

> 1 pink grapefruit, peeled
>
> 3 handfuls spinach
>
> 3 asparagus spears
>
> 2 celery sticks
>
> ½ teaspoon chlorella powder

Juice the fruit and vegetables, and then stir in the chlorella powder. Serve immediately.

Fruit Kale

If you didn't think you liked green juices, think again — with tangy orange and apples, this green juice is sweet and tasty. Alfalfa sprouts may be tiny, but they are power-packed with nutrients. They contain around 3.8 per cent protein and 870mg potassium per 100g, as well as a good supply of B vitamins — making them a great addition in juices for vitality.

1 orange, roughly peeled

2 apples

3 handfuls kale

1 small handful alfalfa sprouts

½ teaspoon barley grass powder

Juice all the fruit and vegetables, and then stir in the barley grass powder. Serve immediately.

Bouncing B Vits

Potatoes, broccoli and strawberries are all sources of B-Complex vitamins, the vitamins needed to turn glucose into energy, so this juice will have you bouncing around in no time! Strawberries are among the top 20 fruits for their antioxidant capacity and a good source of potassium, the mineral electrolyte that plays a vital role in regulating fluid levels in the body, managing blood pressure and keeping the heart functioning properly – perhaps no coincidence then that the strawberry is heart-shaped?

1 potato

1 orange, roughly peeled

3–4 broccoli florets

10–12 strawberries (reserve a slice for decoration)

1 apple

Juice all the ingredients, mix well and serve in an ice-filled glass with a slice of strawberry for decoration.

Sweet Orange Pots

This may seem odd but yes, you can juice sweet potatoes and the result is surprisingly creamy and good! Sweet potatoes not only have more colour than regular potatoes (they are not botanically related), but also they are more nutritious, being rich in vitamins C, beta-carotene, calcium and potassium. Juicing with pineapple gives a sweet, creamy juice that is also rich in B vitamins, the nutrients needed for energy production.

½ sweet potato

1 thick slice fresh pineapple, skin removed

1 orange, roughly peeled

½ teaspoon ginseng powder

Juice the sweet potato and fruit, and then stir in the ginseng powder. Serve over ice.

Running Radishes

Radish juice is quite spicy and strong, so combining with potato and carrot makes it more palatable. Radish juice is thought to aid digestion and is a good source of vitamin C, beta-carotene and vitamin B6, as well as the minerals potassium, calcium, folic acid and manganese.

2 radishes

1 celery stick

1 beetroot

1 carrot

½ medium sweet potato

Juice all the ingredients, stir together and then serve.

– 7 –

Juicing
for life

Juicing is so much more than a health kick or a means to shed pounds or encourage radiant skin – it's also the perfect culinary strategy for improving the nutrition of children or elderly members of the family. In fact anyone who is picky about their food, who has a smaller appetite or finds it more difficult to chew or swallow, or whose digestive system is not working optimally can benefit from the goodness of drinking nutrient-rich fresh juices.

Children are notorious for not eating their greens (or any vegetables in some cases!) so making them colourful juices can help to ensure they get the nutrients they need. And as always with trying to feed children, it's about making it fun and interesting, so juices in crazy shades could be a great way of getting their nutrients in. The key to a healthy child is a strong immune system, to fight disease-producing organisms such as viruses, bacteria and parasites. Very often nutritional deficiencies are the reason for children having chronic immune problems and this is because it is easier for bacteria or viruses to invade and thrive when vital nutrients are missing. Important nutrients needed for a strong immune system include vitamins A, C, D, E and the minerals manganese, selenium, zinc, iron, calcium and magnesium.

Regardless of age, we all need to have a good digestive system and for this to function optimally our gut needs to be colonised by beneficial bacteria that help fight infection. Not only do these bacteria defend our bodies, they also nourish us by producing vitamins B1, B2, B5, B6, K and essential fatty acids, antioxidants and amino acids. Many strains of bacteria also produce enzymes that help break down food. Nutrients in foods that have been fermented with bacteria cultures, such as yogurt, miso or sauerkraut, are more likely to be readily absorbed than nutrients in non-fermented versions of the same ingredients – for example, milk, soy or cabbage.

Incorporating probiotics or prebiotics in our diet may offer some health benefits as they can change the bacterial balance in the body by increasing and supporting the kind of helpful bacteria that can destroy or reduce infection. The first, probiotics, are available in powder or capsule form and in products such as yogurt, dairy drinks and infant formulas to which specific probiotic cultures have been added. What is important is the number of beneficial organisms – and the strain – as certain strains appear to be helpful only for certain conditions. The table overleaf lists examples of a few beneficial bacteria-boosting strains. Unlike probiotics, prebiotics are not digested, they simply pass through the body, acting as 'food' for healthy bacteria in the gut. As well as improving calcium absorption, they also support both digestive and immune health. High concentrations of the prebiotic fructo-oligosaccharides (FOS) can be found in chicory root, asparagus, leeks, onion, Jerusalem artichokes, peas and lentils. Both probiotics and prebiotics can be purchased in capsule form. These are fragile organisms and need to be kept cool to be effective and survive, so make sure you buy capsules that are stored in a refrigerated cabinet. Most good health stores will stock them.

Strain	Action	Used for	Dosage
Fructo-oligosaccharides (FOS) prebiotic	Prebiotic (food for friendly bacteria in the gut)	Diarrhoea or constipation	2,000–3,000mg per day with meals
Bifidobacterium lactis probiotic	Restores gut microflora	Diarrhoea	1–3 billion live organisms per day
Lactobacillus acidophilus probiotic	Creates acidic environment to discourage growth of harmful microorganisms	Strengthening immune system and fighting yeast infection	1 billion live organisms per day
Lactobacillus acidophilus CL 1285 probiotic	Contributes healthy bacteria to the gut	General digestive aid	1 billion live organisms per day
Lactobacillus acidophilus DDS-1 probiotic	Produces lactase enzyme	Lactose intolerance	1 billion live organisms per day
Lactobacillus reuteri RC-14 probiotic	Inhibits growth of harmful bacteria and yeast	Yeast infection	5–10 billion live organisms per day
Saccharomyces boulardii probiotic	Promotes healthy gut flora	Diarrhoea	5–10 billion live organisms – 4 times a day

A good intake of nutrients is just as important in later life, not only for our immune systems but also for bone health. Osteoporosis is a major health issue for older people, particularly women. This condition takes hold when bone density decreases, raising the risk of fractures, so making sure the diet includes calcium-rich foods, such as leafy green vegetables is important. vitamin D helps us to absorb calcium so as well as increasing your intake of eggs and oily fish, this is another reason to get outside and stroll in the sunshine.

Recent research shows a link between the increasing incidence of dementia in the elderly and poor nutrition. Age-related decline in brain function can start as early as 45, but nutrients (or rather the lack of nutrients) that can affect cognitive decline include omega-3 fatty acids, antioxidants such as vitamin E (important because of the inflammatory nature of Alzheimer's disease), B vitamins and acetylcholine, which is a key part of memory function. It is therefore just as necessary to maintain a diet that is high in micronutrients right through life.

Mad Melon

This is a great sweet juice with 'hidden' broccoli that your child will never notice. Broccoli is rich in vitamins A, C, E and K, beneficial for growing bones, as well as B vitamins and chromium, which is useful for digestion. For optimum effect, sprinkle in a capsule of probiotics to help support their immune system too.

¼ of a small cantaloupe melon, peeled (plus extra for decoration)

¼ sweet potato

a few broccoli florets

Juice all the ingredients and serve immediately, adding a small wedge of melon for decoration.

Juice on the Move

Being constipated and unable to rid the body of toxins and cellular waste matter can have a detrimental effect on many systems in the body, so it's important to treat this condition, and one of the easiest ways is through juicing. The best juices are from fruits that are high in fibre or sorbitol, a naturally occurring sugar that is not digested well and helps to soften stools. Adding psyllium husks and increasing your intake of water may also be beneficial. This sweet juice is perfect for young and old alike.

1 apple

1 pear

1 plum

1 small handful raspberries

1 carrot

Juice all the ingredients and mix together before drinking.

1. Brain Food
2. Super Green
3. Beneficial Bug Boost
4. Gazpacho Juice

Brain Food

Feeding the brain is important throughout life, not just as we age. One of the easiest ways to recognise nutrition deficiency is from a change in mental functioning, and this applies to poor hydration too – just 2 per cent dehydration can affect both mental and physical performance – another reason to drink lots of great juices. This one is rich in antioxidants, while the addition of chia oil gives a small boost of healthy omega fats too.

> 1 small handful blueberries
>
> 1 orange, roughly peeled
>
> 1 carrot
>
> 3–4 broccoli florets
>
> 1 teaspoon chia oil

Juice all the fruit and vegetables, and then stir in the chia oil before serving.

Super Green

Although this is green, it is sweet and full of flavour that children will like, so it's a great juice for a boost of vegetables – not many children will eat spinach and celery knowingly! The pineapple will provide a little digestive support, whilst spinach and parsley are both rich in many vitamins and minerals that a growing body needs.

> 1 small handful parsley
>
> 1 celery stick
>
> 1 small handful baby spinach leaves
>
> 1 tangerine, peeled
>
> 1 cm slice fresh pineapple, peeled, plus a wedge to decorate

Juice all the ingredients and serve poured over ice with a wedge of pineapple for decoration.

Beneficial Bug Boost

This juice includes some prebiotic-rich foods (Jerusalem artichokes and garlic) that help to 'feed' your friendly bacteria. Jerusalem artichokes are not really artichokes and do not come from Jerusalem – they originated from North America and are tubers, often called sunchokes, as they are a variety of the sunflower. Their flavour is similar to potato, but a bit nutty, and they are known to cause bad flatulence in some people, although juicing doesn't seem to have the same effect!

1 small Jerusalem artichoke

1 garlic clove

3–4 broccoli florets

2cm piece fresh ginger root, peeled

2 carrots

Juice all the ingredients together, and then stir and serve.

Gazpacho Juice

If you like gazpacho soup you will just love this juice, as it has all the same ingredients; you just don't need a spoon! Rich in colour, it is also rich in nutrients. Tomatoes and red peppers both contain high levels of the carotenoid lycopene, a powerful phytonutrient that functions as an antioxidant to help protect against degenerative diseases, sunburn and skin damage. The garlic in this juice is entirely optional, but remember it is a great source of antioxidants, very cleansing for the skin and a useful anti-inflammatory.

1 red pepper, seeds removed

1 tomato

½ cucumber

1 garlic clove (optional)

1 small handful basil leaves

1 teaspoon extra virgin olive oil

freshly milled black pepper, to serve

Juice all the vegetables with the basil leaves, and then stir in the olive oil. Serve with a sprinkling of freshly milled black pepper, if liked.

Strawberries on the Beat

Another juice that can be given to children who are adverse to eating vegetables. The strong flavour of the strawberries will cover the fact that a little beetroot and carrot has gone into this drink, with the added benefit of all the nutrients they provide. Beetroot is known for its antioxidant, anti-inflammatory and detoxification benefits, but you may want to warn children about their wee turning pink after drinking too much of this – something my own children find hilarious!

8–10 strawberries, one to decorate

2 carrots

1 small beetroot

1 small handful mint leaves

Juice all the ingredients and mix together. Pour over ice and serve with a whole strawberry.

Bouncing Bones

This juice is rich in calcium, a mineral that is very important to bone health. But calcium is also needed for the heart, muscles and nerves to function properly, and for blood to clot, so this juice is not just for the elderly. Vitamin D plays an important role in protecting bones, and the body requires it to absorb calcium. Vitamin D occurs naturally in only a very few foods – eggs and oily fish (such as mackerel, herring and salmon, for example – however it is also added to some brands of foods. One of the best ways to get your daily intake is from a little sunshine.

1 small handful watercress

1 apple

¼ cucumber

a few broccoli florets

1 kiwi fruit, peeled

Juice all the ingredients and stir well before serving.

– 8 –

Juicy
foods

Juicing doesn't have to be only for drinking juices, as there are lots of ways of incorporating the juice you've made in solid foods too. As juices can be strong in flavour, they are great used in salad dressings, soups, children's ice lollies, plus many other quick and easy recipes. If you want to add a little more flavour to your gravy to accompany a roast, why not juice a few herbs with fresh horseradish, carrots and celery to give it a fresh, light herb taste with a bit of heat? Or make your own version of a non-alcoholic mulled cocktail by juicing your favourite fruits and then warming them gently with a few spices such as cloves, star anise and cinnamon sticks?

Obviously, we're not only adding flavour here, this is also a great way to add extra nutrients to our food. Be conscious, though, of not heating the juices too much or some of those important nutrients may be lost. This actually applies to cooking in general, the more gently you cook your food the more likely you are to retain that nutrient content – so light steaming is preferable to high-heat frying. And you don't need to waste the pulp! Obviously if you have a composter or wormery this will go on to make great compost, but the pulp can also be included as a tasty, nutritious addition in many other recipes, such as cakes, biscuits, burgers and even bread.

> Ideally juices should be drunk half an hour or more before meals. If drunk after a meal, the sugars and starches in the juice could start to ferment in the digestive tract while the other food is still being digested, which could lead to digestive upsets.

Blackberry Jelly

A gorgeous deep purple jelly, full of fruit and flavour. Be careful not to heat the juice too much during cooking, as this may reduce the great nutrients from the fruit. This makes a delicious dessert, especially if you can gather your own blackberries.

Serves 2

1 large handful blackberries

2 large handfuls red grapes

1 teaspoon honey

3 leaves gelatine (or vegetarian agar)

8–10 blackberries, kept whole

Juice the fruits – you want about 400ml juice.

Pour half the juice into a pan with the honey and the remainder into a bowl with the gelatine leaves and set aside to soak for 5 minutes.

Gently heat the juice in the pan, adding the gelatine and remaining juice after a couple of minutes. Stir until the gelatine has completely dissolved.

Divide the remaining blackberries between 2 small bowls or glasses, and then pour in the warm liquid. Chill in the fridge until set.

Orange Granita

This fruity sorbet is a perfect summer dessert, served either on its own, or with fresh strawberries.

Serves 4

3–4 oranges (you need 500ml juice)

220g golden caster sugar

300ml water

Juice the oranges.

Place the sugar in a small pan with the water and heat over a low heat, stirring, until the sugar has dissolved. Leave to cool.

Mix together the sugar syrup and orange juice, pour into a freezerproof container and freeze for 4 hours, or until set.

To serve, rake with a fork and spoon into glasses or over fresh fruit.

Carrot and Orange Muffins

Another great way to get healthy fruit and vegetables into children! Juicing the fruit and vegetables but then adding back the pulp gives great fibre to these tasty muffins. You can also use a mix of wholemeal and white flour if preferred. These delicious muffins are also dairy-free.

Makes 10–12

1 carrot

1 orange, roughly peeled

75g raisins

100g dark muscovado sugar

2 eggs

3 tablespoons sunflower oil

75g desiccated coconut

200g wholemeal self-raising flour

½ teaspoon ground cinnamon

pinch nutmeg

Preheat the oven to 180°C/gas mark 4 and line a 12-hole muffin tin with paper cases.

Juice the carrot and orange, reserving the pulp. Put the raisins into a small bowl and pour over the juice. Leave to stand.

Whisk together the sugar and eggs in a large bowl until smooth and creamy. Slowly whisk in the oil then add the remaining ingredients, including the raisins, juice and pulp. Mix well but do not over-mix.

Drop a tablespoonful of the mixture into each paper case then bake for 20–22 minutes, until risen and golden.

Leave to cool on a rack before eating.

Chilled Avocado Soup

This is a real summer favourite – creamy avocados with a hint of lime and garlic, topped with a lightly boiled egg. Rich in healthy fats, the avocado is also a source of anti-inflammatory carotenoids that lie in the dark green flesh just beneath the skin, so be sure to scrape this out thoroughly.

Serves 2

6 tomatoes

¾ cucumber

½ lime, unpeeled

2 garlic cloves

1 large avocado, stoned and peeled

freshly milled black pepper, to taste

to serve

1 lightly boiled egg, peeled and halved

avocado oil

Juice together the tomatoes, ½ the cucumber, lime and garlic.

Pour the juice into a blender and add the avocado flesh. Process until smooth, taste and add pepper if required. Chill for 30 minutes.

Dice the remaining cucumber.

Divide the soup between 2 bowls and top each one with half a boiled egg. To serve, sprinkle with the diced cucumber and finish with a drizzle of avocado oil.

Citrus Salad Dressing

Salad dressings are simple to make, and using citrus fruits adds a kick of vitamin C to your diet too. This recipe makes a large amount that can be kept in the fridge and used whenever you need it. Leave a little of the peel on the fruits for a sharper, stronger flavour. When making a salad dressing it's good to taste as you go, so you can add more or less of the flavours you like.

Serves 4–6 people

1 lime, roughly peeled

1 lemon, roughly peeled

1cm piece fresh ginger root, peeled

2 garlic cloves

6–9 tablespoons extra virgin olive oil

2 teaspoons wholegrain mustard

1 teaspoon honey

freshly milled black pepper

Juice the lime, lemon, ginger and garlic.

Gradually whisk in the oil – the ratio should be three times the amount of oil to juice. Finally, whisk in the mustard and honey, and season to taste.

Pour into a container and keep in the fridge until needed.

Traffic Light Lollies

No child will be able to resist these fun lollies – they're packed with vitamins yet delicious and very simple to make. Vary the fruits to include those that your children love. My small ones find this particular combo irresistible.

Makes 6

8 strawberries

½–1 teaspoon honey

1 orange, roughly peeled

2 peaches, stoned

1 apple

2 kiwi, peeled

6 lolly sticks

Juice the strawberries and taste for sweetness, adding a little honey if needed. Pour into 6 ice-lolly moulds and freeze for 4 hours until set.

Juice the orange, and then blend the juice with the peaches in a blender or food processor. Remove the lolly moulds from the freezer and pour the peach mixture on top of the frozen strawberry mixture. Stick the lolly sticks in the moulds and freeze for a further 4 hours.

Juice the apple, and then blend the juice with the kiwi fruit in a blender or food processor. Pour into the moulds and freeze for a further 4 hours.

To serve, dip the moulds into warm water to remove the lollies.

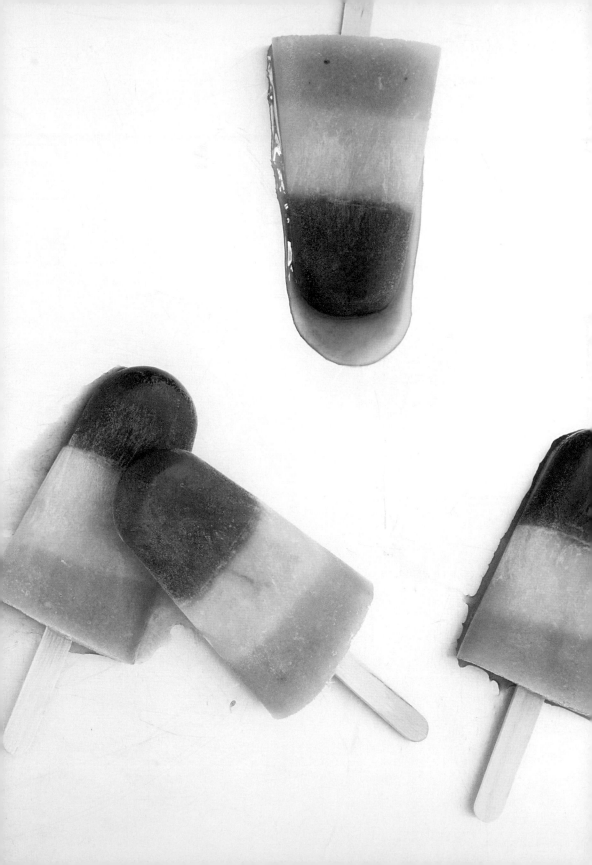

Stunning Smoothie

Smoothies can be a healthy snack, but all too often they contain too much fruit and therefore are full of sugar (especially the shop-bought ones). Here is a simple way of getting a few more nutrients into your smoothie, but without missing out on great taste. This smoothie is made with beetroot, but you could vary the vegetable juice depending on which nutrients you want to increase in your diet. This is also an ideal way of getting children to take in more vegetable juice! The almonds add a little creaminess, they are rich in calcium and a good source of protein.

Serves 1

1 small beetroot

1 banana, peeled

1 small handful raspberries

1 tablespoon ground almonds

150ml milk

Juice the beetroot.

Put the beetroot juice, banana, raspberries, almonds and milk into a blender or food processor and blend until smooth.

Beetroot Crackers

Using the pulp from your juicing is a great way to get more fibre into your diet. These crackers can be made with different pulps, depending on the juices you have made – some pulp is more moist than others and obviously this also depends on your particular juicer as some yield more juice than others. The pulp can be 'baked' in a dehydrator if you have one, in the lowest oven of an Aga or in a very low-heat oven.

Makes 10–12

75g beetroot pulp
(or pulp of your choice)

75g chia seeds

75g ground almonds

1 teaspoon celery seeds

50g sesame seeds

25g ground linseeds

1 teaspoon salt

½ teaspoon freshly milled
black pepper

1 egg

50ml water

Preheat the oven to 120°C/gas mark ½.

Put the pulp into a large bowl and mix in all the seeds and seasoning.

Whisk the egg and water together in a measuring jug, and then stir into the seed mixture to make a loose dough.

Spread the dough onto a lightly greased baking sheet, pressing it down to about 2mm thickness. Cut into squares, and then bake in the oven for 2 hours.

Remove from the oven and cool on a rack.

Feel-good foods

The World Health Organization recommends we should eat about 500g of fruit and vegetables (excluding potatoes) every day to keep fit and healthy. This means at least five portions, but the average British diet includes only about half that amount. The Greeks and Spanish eat at least twice the amount of vegetables as most British people and this higher vegetable consumption is part of the so-called 'Mediterranean diet effect' hailed as being responsible for lower rates of cancer and heart disease in Mediterranean countries. So the message is: for better health, go for *at least* five portions of fruit and vegetables every day.

By making fresh fruit and vegetable juices part of your daily diet you can easily meet that WHO recommendation. A combined eating plan of juices and light, nutritious meals will stimulate the body to eliminate toxins and repair damaged cells, as well as curbing your appetite – so it should help you to lose weight too. The combination of juice and food also ensures adequate fibre in your diet and studies worldwide have shown that fibre plays a key role in preventing colon cancer – another reason why many health experts suggest we eat 'around a juicer', meaning we should be eating plenty of high-fibre foods such as fruit and vegetables, whole grains and legumes, as well as drinking juices.

Daily juicing along with healthier eating

- flushes out waste matter
- provides fluid to the cells
- replaces depleted vitamins and minerals
- builds up stores of nutrients for later
- assists with regular bowel and urine function

The one-week wellbeing eating plan

Here's my own simple and basic guide to what you can and can't eat on this one-week wellbeing eating plan, which combines fresh fruit and vegetable juices with healthy meals. As with all roads to better health, adding daily exercise, correct breathing and posture, and a positive attitude are also beneficial for your wellbeing.

Almost all of us will benefit from incorporating fresh juice into our daily diet. It's so easy to do, too – have a juice instead of a cup of coffee or tea in the morning, or in place of that first glass of wine in the evening. If you are at home during the day you could have a juice pick-me-up mid-morning or mid-afternoon. Once you start juicing – and once you start to see and feel the benefits – it will become a way of life that you won't want to give up.

Here's to a healthier and more beautiful you!

Include:

- 1–3 fresh fruit or vegetable juices per day
- 1–2 litres bottled or pure, filtered water per day
- Herb tea: camomile, dandelion, fennel, peppermint, etc.

Breakfast ideas

Fruit salad

Stewed fruit or, out of season, a compote made from dried fruits

Prunes

Plain, organic, live yogurt
(served with any of the above)

Porridge with raisins or stewed apple

Herb teas

Hot water with lemon and ginger

And when all else fails... grab a piece of fresh fruit – even a banana or apple munched on the run is better than no breakfast at all

Lunch ideas

Raw vegetable salad with Citrus Salad Dressing, page 179

Baked potato or steamed potatoes in their skins

Brown rice, wild rice or brown Basmati rice

Sprouted seeds and beans

Vegetable soup

Avocado

Cottage cheese (preferably organic)

Fruit

Supper ideas

Fresh fish – grilled or baked

Rye bread and tahini (sesame paste)

Sweet potato – steamed

Baked potato

Vegetable stew with lentils or beans

Wholegrain organic brown rice, quinoa or millet

Lightly cooked vegetables (preferably steamed)

Steamed or (very) lightly stir-fried vegetables in rapeseed or olive oil, served still crunchy

Salads with olive oil dressing

Snacks

Rye bread

Vegetable crudités

Pumpkin seeds, sunflower seeds, whole almonds in their skins

Dried fruit: bananas or apricots (preferably unsulphured)

Unsweetened cocoa nibs

Foods to limit/avoid

Meat (especially processed meats, such as pork products and bacon)

Cream and cheese (only cottage cheese is allowed for this one week!)

A little organic (preferably grass-fed) milk and butter is fine

Wheat: bread, pastry, cakes, biscuits

Damaged, artificial fats such as margarine and low-fat spreads

Sugar and excess salt (try a squeeze of fresh lemon juice instead of the salt shaker)

Tea, coffee, alcohol

Processed foods

Highly fried food

Useful Addresses

SUPPLIERS

Naturya

Excellent range of some of my favourite powdered superfoods (wheat grass, barley grass, chlorella, spirulina and more) available from leading health-food shops. Soil Association certified organic. Highly recommended.

www.naturya.com

Pukka Herbs

Excellent range of unusual organically grown herbs and herb teas, including Fibre Plus powder with linseed and aloe vera – useful for adding to juice blends – as well as the more usual organic wheat grass and other super-food powders.

www.pukkaherbs.com

Victoria Health

Web-based purveyors of a wide range of useful food supplements and interesting ingredients for juicers, such as liquid chlorella drops.

www.victoriahealth.com

Revital

Online sales for brands such as LifeStream (from America) and numerous green food powders.

www.revital.co.uk

ORGANISATIONS

British Naturopathic Association

1 Green Lane Avenue
Street
Somerset BA16 0QS

www.naturopaths.org.uk

The professional body of practising naturopaths who are registered with the General Council and Register of Naturopaths in the UK. An excellent naturopathy resource and information centre.

Gerson Institute

4631 Viewridge Avenue
San Diego
California CA 92123
USA

www.gerson.org

A non-profit cancer clinic and alternative treatment centre for chronic degenerative diseases founded in 1977 by Charlotte Gerson, daughter of Dr Max Gerson. Focus is on juice therapy.

Register of Integrative Colon Therapists and Trainers

17 North Town Road
Maidenhead
Berkshire
SL6 7JQ

www.colonic-association.net

An excellent resource to find qualified colon therapists both in the UK and worldwide.

The Soil Association

South Plaza
Marlborough Street
Bristol BS1 3NX

Soil Association Scotland
18C Liberton Brae
Tower Mains
Edinburgh EH16 6AE

www.soilassociation.org

Britain's leading resource centre for all things organic, food and farming-wise. An excellent resource for news updates, suppliers of organic produce and information on a wide range of organic food and farming issues. Soil Association-certified organic produce is widely considered to be the 'gold standard' in terms of integrity and quality.

Wholistic Research Company

Unit 1, Five House Farm Business Park
Sandon Road
Therfield
Royston
Hertfordshire SG8 9RE

www.wholisticresearch.com

Interesting and unusual website selling professional range of juicers, including the Champion and Hurom professional ranges. Many more resources for the serious juicer, including specialist books, grain and seed mills, sprouters, enema kits, water distillers and more!

The Institute for Complementary and Natural Medicine

Can-Mezzanine
32–36 Loman Street
London SE1 0EH

www.icnm.org.uk

The ICNM is a charity set up to inform the public about Complementary and Natural Medicine (CAM) and to administer a multi-disciplinary register of professional practitioners and therapists. It will provide a list of practitioners in your area and details of a wide range of courses, lectures and events in the fields of nutrition and naturopathy.

5:2 diets 85

acai powder 81
acid/alkaline balance 16, 33, 41–2, 66, 70, 75
adaptogens 135
additives 12
Advanced Glycation End products 115
advantages of juicing 16, 186
ageing 26, 28, 31, 50, 90, 114–15
alfalfa sprouts 26, 77, 143
allergies 26, 47, 50, 67, 89–90
amino acids 16, 26, 30–1
anthocyanins 13, 28, 114
antioxidants 13, 15, 16, 28–31, 114, 134
apple 61, 102, 108, 116, 120, 124, 128, 136, 140, 143, 144, 157, 164, 180
apricot 65
arthritis 11, 28, 42, 49, 59, 64, 70, 72, 75
asparagus 43, 102, 108, 124, 140
avocado 124
    avocado chilled soup 176–7

barley grass 80–1, 134–5, 143
baths, Epsom Salts 91–5
battery charge 138
beauty 12
beetroot 44, 109, 146, 162, 182
    beetroot beat-the-blues 139
    beetroot crackers 184–5
    beety energiser 136–7
beneficial bug boost 158–9, 161
beta-carotene 30
bioflavonoids 30
blackberry 68, 128
    blackberry jelly 170–1
blood pressure 10, 42, 68
blood sugar levels 13, 68, 75, 102, 108, 115
blueberry 127, 128, 139, 160
bouncing B vits 144–5
bouncing bones 164–5
brain
    brain food 158, 160
    brain function 152, 160
breakfasts 187
broccoli 45, 123, 144, 154, 160, 161, 164
broccoli sprouts 120
bromelain 41

buying food 37, 39

cabbage 46, 104
    cool cabbage 110–11
calcium 24, 164
cancer 10–11, 18, 21, 28, 31–3, 43, 45, 54–5, 57, 59, 62–4, 68, 70, 77, 86–7, 186
cardiovascular disease 11, 28, 31, 59, 68, 87, 186
carrot 57, 101, 108, 110, 116, 120, 124, 136, 138, 140, 146, 157, 160, 162
    and orange muffins 174–5
celery 42, 108, 109, 110, 130, 140, 146, 160
cellulite 15, 18, 90
cherry 128
chia oil 116, 160
children 150–64
chlorella 80–1, 124, 134–5, 139, 140
chlorophyll 16, 26
cinnamon 102, 174
citric acid 13–15, 52, 54
citrus roots 116–17
citrus salad dressing 178–9
clean and green 140–1
co-factors 19
coenzyme 110 114
coffee 91
colds and flu 40, 49, 52, 53, 54, 59, 61, 64, 74, 76
complexion calmer 124–5
constipation 41, 66, 72, 85, 94, 152, 157
coriander 77, 101
crackers, beetroot 184–5
cranberry 74
cucumber 56, 108, 110, 119, 124, 127, 161, 164, 176

dandelion 73
'dead food' 12, 19
dementia 152
detoxification 15, 18, 61, 89, 90, 91, 98, 162
diabetes 10, 11, 87, 115
digestion 11–13, 16, 18–19, 26, 41–2, 44, 50, 53, 55–7, 63, 67–8, 68, 71, 71–2, 86–7, 91, 98–9, 108, 110, 127, 146, 151, 154, 160, 169
disease 10, 11, 20, 86, 151
    see also specific diseases

diuretics 55, 67, 73, 74, 77, 84, 102
dry skin brushing 91–2, 94

eating plan, one-week wellbeing 186–7
elderly people 150–64
elimination diets 43, 54, 67, 75, 92–4
endive 51
enemas 91–3
energy, juicing for 135–47
enzyme attack 103
enzymes 12, 16, 18–19, 20, 41, 50, 103
Epsom Salts baths 91–5
equipment 36
essential fatty acids 114–15

fasting 19, 85–7, 89–95
fennel 58, 124
fertilisers 12, 37
fibre 11, 13
flax seed oil 119, 127, 128
folic acid 23, 72
food production 10–11, 12, 31
foods to avoid/limit 187
free radicals 28, 30, 114, 134
'French paradox' 75
fructo-oligosaccharides (FOS) 151–2

garlic 130, 138, 161, 176, 179
gazpacho juice 158–9, 161
Gerson Therapy diet 21, 28, 32, 86
ginger root 76, 110, 120, 122–4, 136, 139, 161, 179
ginseng 135, 144
glycation 115
GM-crops 38
gout 33, 70, 72
granita, orange 172–3
grape 13–14, 75, 122, 128, 170
grapefruit 53, 140
green dream cleaning machine 106
greenie genie 124–5
gut bacteria 50, 151–2, 161

haemoglobin 134
hair 25, 43, 47, 49, 56, 60, 63–4, 87, 89, 90
health 11
hemp 80–1
herbs 77

immune system 151, 154
Inner Cleansing Juice Diet 89–90
iron deficiency 25

jelly, blackberry 170–1
Jerusalem artichoke 161
'juice drinks' 12
juice manufacturers 12
juice on the move 156–7
juice-fasting 19, 87, 89–95
   one-day 91–2
   optional extras 94–5
   three-day 93
juicers 36

kale 47, 120
   fruit kale 142–3
   kale and hearty 106–7, 109
kiwi fruit 40, 120, 164, 180

Lactobacillus 152
laxatives 46, 50, 66–7, 84, 157
leek, luscious lean 101
lemon 52, 109, 110, 136, 179
lemon grass 116
lettuce 51, 60, 127
lime 52, 101, 103, 108, 116, 120, 130, 176, 179
linseed 92–4
local produce 39
lollies, traffic light 180–1
lunches 187

maca powder 135, 138
macronutrients 134
malic acid 13–15
mango 62
'Mediterranean diet effect' 186
melon 55, 119, 123
   mad melon 154–5
   melon cocktail 123
menstrual disturbances 25, 44, 58, 68
metabolism 11, 18, 53, 63, 75, 89–90, 104, 115, 134
micro-antioxidants 30–1
micronutrients 20, 134
mineral deficiency 25
minerals 20–1, 24–5, 30–1, 134
mint 103, 104, 136, 162
   summer mint 118–19

muffin, carrot and orange 174–5

nails 25, 49, 64
nutritional deficiency 11, 20, 25, 151, 160

omega-3s/omega-6s 114–15
orange 54, 138, 139, 143, 144, 160, 180
   and carrot muffins 174–5
   granita 172–3
organic produce 31, 37, 39, 70–1, 75
osteoporosis 46, 152

papaya 50, 102
parsley 108, 109, 120, 124, 130, 140, 160
   punch 140–1
parsnip 64, 116
peach 66, 180
pear 67, 157
pepper 49, 120, 161
pesticides 12, 37–9, 70–1, 75
phytonutrients 134
pineapple 13, 41, 103, 108, 144, 160
plum 157
plumper skin perfecter 128–9
polyphenols 74–5
potato 71, 116, 144
prebiotics 151–2, 161
pregnancy 23, 72, 87
probiotics 151–2
protein 26, 30–1, 99
prunes 66
psyllium husks 92–4, 99, 109

radish 67
   running radishes 146–7
raspberry 68, 157, 182
   spiced 122
raw foods 18, 84, 86
Recommended Daily Allowances (RDAs) 20–5
refined foods 10, 33
retinol 30

salad dressing, citrus 178–9
selenium 30–1
sickness 76
skin 6–7, 12–13, 16, 47, 49, 51, 52, 61, 63–4, 71, 87, 89, 90, 95, 113–31
   skin soother 126–7

skin sunrise 120–1
smoothies 13
   stunning 182–3
snacks 187
soup, chilled avocado 176–7
spicy spears 102
spinach 72, 108, 140, 160
spirulina 80–1, 120, 124, 134–5
sprouted seeds/beans 26, 77, 120, 143
sprouting greens 120
stomach conditions 42, 45–6, 50, 58, 71, 84
strawberry 59, 104–5, 144, 180
   on the beat 162–3
sugar 10
sulphur-rich foods 98
summer slimmer 104–5
super green 158, 160
suppers 187
sweet potato 144, 146, 154
Swiss chard 108

tangerine 160
tartaric acid 13–15
Thermic Effect of Food (TEF) 18
tomato 70, 101, 130, 161, 176
toxins 16, 18, 40, 73, 86–7, 89–90, 92–4, 98, 157
turnip 48

unjuiceables 40

Virgin Mary 130–1
vitality 32, 86
vitamin A 22, 30
vitamin B complex 22–3, 134, 144
vitamin C 23, 28, 30, 54
vitamin D 164
vitamin deficiency 20
vitamin E 22, 30
vitamins 20–3, 28, 30, 134

water intake 135
watercress 63, 122, 164
   watercress wonder 106, 108
watermelon 55, 123
weight loss 16, 75, 85, 86, 87, 90, 97–110
'Western' diet 10
wheat grass 77–8, 124, 134–5, 140

Acknowledgements

Many special people have helped me produce this beautiful book, including the talented team at Kyle Books. I would like to thank Sophie Allen and Kyle Cathie herself for such continued support and enthusiasm for my Wellbeing publishing projects. Also our book designer Sinem Erkas and copy editor Stephanie Evans, as well as recipe consultant Joy Skipper for working with me to create some of the most delicious new juicing recipes. A special thanks to the gorgeous Georgia Glynn-Smith for so many wonderful and inspiring juice pictures, so ably assisted by food stylist Emily Jonzen and prop stylist Tamzin Ferdinando. A big thanks to Patrick Drummond and his assistant Charlie Lyons for his portraits of me, the children and much more besides. And to Lily Earle, also known as the blogger Deeper Dazzle for her beauty and grace on these pages. On the subject of beauty, my gratitude goes to Christopher Noulton for his wonderful illustrations which look so wonderful on the page. Last, but not least, grateful thanks to Polly Beard, Annabelle Hill and my entire 'Top Team' at Liz Earle Wellbeing. Thank You!

Twitter: @LizEarleWb
Instagram: @lizearlewellbeing
Facebook: Liz Earle Wellbeing
Pinterest: Liz Earle Wellbeing